COMPUTER:
The Mind Stretcher

WEYMAN JONES

COMPUTER: The Mind Stretcher

Foreword by Christopher C. Kraft

Diagrams by Nicholas Costantino

The Dial Press, Inc.   New York

To Lynn and Paula

who will come to know the computer
as well as they know the TV

CONTENTS

Weyman Jones has written a book that will help those interested in computers to understand some of the fundamentals of computer science. Most people tend to look upon computers as devices for use in scientific or engineering areas, but more and more uses are made of computers in other entirely unrelated fields. In his book, Weyman Jones has described a number of examples to show how the computer can be used in almost every business in our land. Although the book is aimed at the young person, the modern businessman will find it will provide him a basic understanding of a machine he must face up to in today's computer world.

The future of every country is based on its competence in technology and science. We have all come to realize that the so-called space race between the United States and Russia has really been only an arena for demonstrating the technological capabilities which each country has achieved. Progress in space activities is followed closely by all nations of the world and is an example of the fact that the nation that stays number one technologically will be looked upon as the world's leader.

At the core of our recent technological advancements is the modern high-speed computer. Without the tremendous advancement in computers which we have seen during the past 25 years, we would still be struggling for the answers to many problems that are now taken for granted. The high-speed computer has been essential to the fantastic progress in our nation's space program during the past ten years. Without these advancements in computers, the flights to the moon and other complex space flight operations planned for the near future would be impossible.

I recommend this book for all those who are interested in understanding one of the most unique and useful tools ever devised by man. I am sure the reader will be inspired to push further in a field of science and technology that will change the nation and the world in ways that even the most sophisticated minds have not yet imagined.

Christopher C. Kraft
DIRECTOR OF FLIGHT OPERATIONS
MANNED SPACECRAFT CENTER, HOUSTON, TEXAS

COMPUTER:
The Mind Stretcher

1
THE PROBLEM-SOLVING MACHINE

"What number are you calling?" the operator says.

You tell her.

Two seconds later the operator says, "That number has been changed," and tells you the new one. Her voice sounds different.

It is.

A computer has looked up the new number and given it to you.

"Touch the hairy animal that has four legs and says meow," the woman's voice says.

On the TV screen is a list of words:

CAR

BIRD

CAT

BALL

FISH

The boy picks up what looks like a pen and touches the word CAT. A spot of light appears on the screen.

"Good," the voice says in his earphones. "Now touch . . ."

He is using a computer to learn to read.

The red eye of the furnace glares at a row of generators that send electricity through miles of wire to all the houses spread along the hills above. Night gathers in the valley and lights go on. Men come home and turn on television for the news. Dinners are cooking on electric stoves. Altogether the houses need more electricity. The furnace dims and then flares orange. Another generator hums into life.

A computer is balancing the production of electricity with the demand.

Masked men in pale green bend over a table under a cold white light. A nurse presses an instrument into a rubber-gloved hand. The surgeon takes a stitch in the living heart of a young woman. Another doctor watches a TV screen in the operating room. He sees the blood pressure beginning to drop and orders a transfusion.

A computer is watching measuring devices attached to the patient and telling the surgical team what is going on inside her.

In a few minutes the electronic computer can finish a job that would take a man his whole lifetime. With the computer we can tackle questions that have always been too big to consider.

Huge rough-cut stones scattered around an empty plain near Wiltshire, England, have puzzled people for centuries. They were obviously hauled there by people long, long ago who placed them in a precise pattern. Why?

Scholars used a computer to plot the daily positions of the sun and the moon 3,500 years ago and discovered that the pattern of stones, called Stonehenge, formed a kind of calendar. Counting the stones, the ancient Britons could predict the seasons.

To understand Stonehenge, thousands of complex calculations were needed, and yet inside any computer only a few very simple things happen. Things like adding one to one and recognizing the difference between plus, minus, and zero.

Computers do complicated jobs by breaking them down into a few simple operations that are done over and over a great many times, but done almost as fast as light. Understanding a computer is mostly just understanding how a few simple operations can be put together in complicated patterns.

Suppose you wanted to find the team batting average of a baseball club. First you would write down each player's batting average to *put* it *into* the problem. Call that "input." Then you would add them up, which is an arithmetic process, and so call that "processing." As you got each number of the sum you would write it down to remember—"memory." Then you would divide the total by the number of players—more "processing." Finally you would *put out* the answer, and so call that "output."

Of course, before you even started you had to know, step by step, how to figure averages. Call that a "program."

Here's a roadmap of that problem:

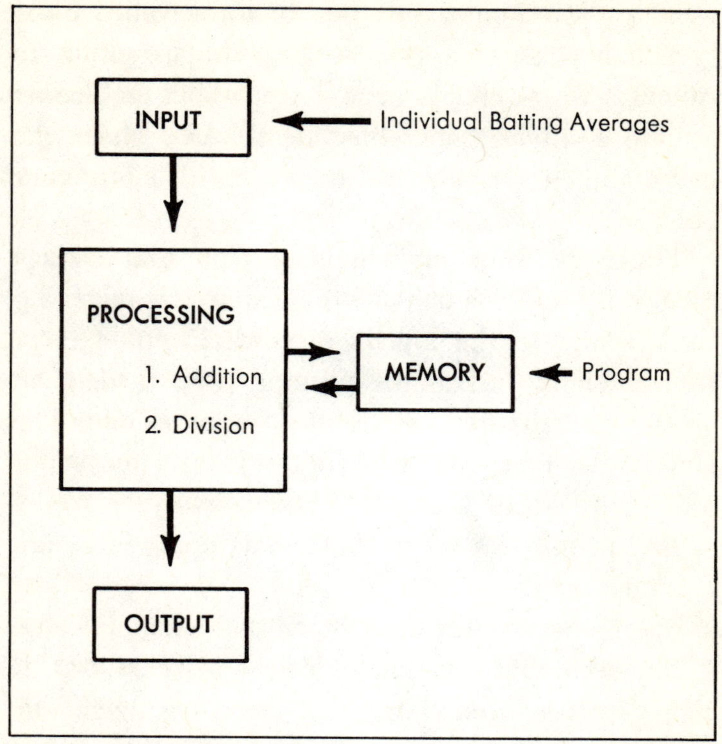

Any problem, no matter how complicated, eventually takes you from input through processing and memory to output. A computer is a problem-solving machine, and so those are the things that go on inside it.

We'll start in the middle, with PROCESSING, to see how it works.

But the story of the computer keeps taking us into the lives of people. It starts with an ancient Chinese, wanders clear around the world to a nineteen-year-old French boy, on to a grouchy Englishman, jumps to America, where people are worrying about an electric cannon and where later they are thinking about the moon and the planets, and then goes right into your life.

There are some inventions of man that change men. For hundreds of years there were few men who could read; after the printing press was invented, there were millions. Just as the printing press made man literate, the gasoline engine made men mobile. The computer is that kind of invention. It does in seconds routine arithmetic that would take a man years to do, so that people can spend those years doing more important work.

But the computer does more than that. Because it can accomplish so much logical work so fast, it allows us to control things that are changing rapidly and to understand the whole shape of things that without the computer we could see only in parts. People are changed by ideas. The computer allows us to shape deeper, broader, and more beautiful ideas, and then the ideas become part of us.

The computer is a machine that is changing you.

2
HOW IT STARTED

The most widely used computer today was not made by IBM or Burroughs or Univac. It wasn't even made in America. It is the Chinese abacus.

The old man in a tea shop in San Francisco today uses an abacus almost exactly like one Marco Polo might have seen in the land he called Cathay seven hundred years ago, and the abacus was already hundreds of years old then.

The abacus is just a step beyond the counting device of the Stone Age: a mark in the sand filled with pebbles that could be pushed back and forth to represent numbers. The Latin word for "pebble" is *calculus*, and pebbles in the sand were probably the second "calculator." (The first was the human hand. Even today we call numbers "digits" from the Latin word *digitus* for "fingers," and "eleven," one more than all our fingers, comes from an old word meaning "and one left over." The computers we're talking about in this book are called digital computers because they work by counting.)

The Chinese invented the abacus by changing the pebbles to flat wooden beads which they strung on wires in a frame.

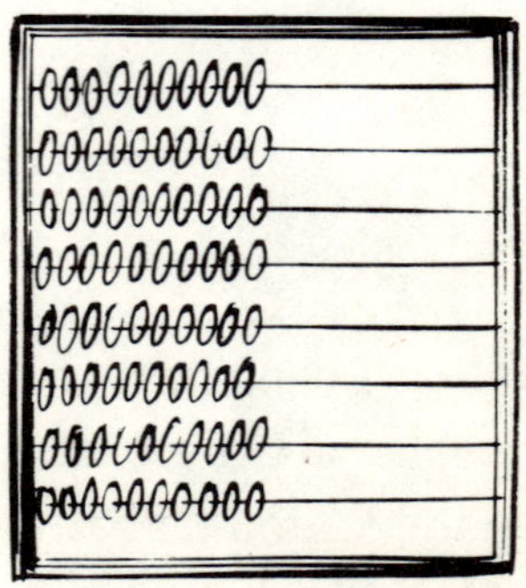

Each wire, like a pair of hands, has ten "digits."

With all the beads pushed to the left there is a space
on the right. To record "one," push a bead to the
right.

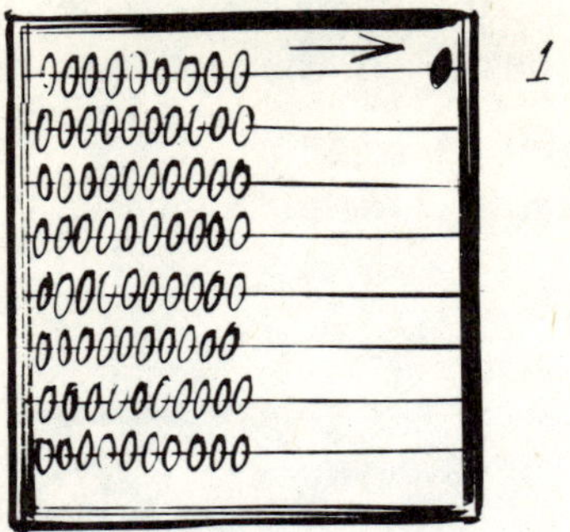

"Two"—another bead, and so on to "ten."

Now watch the old man in front of the tea shop
closely. He doesn't just keep counting off beads from
the row below. Instead, he pushes all the beads on
the first wire back again to the left and moves *one*
bead in the second row to stand for *all ten* first-row
beads.

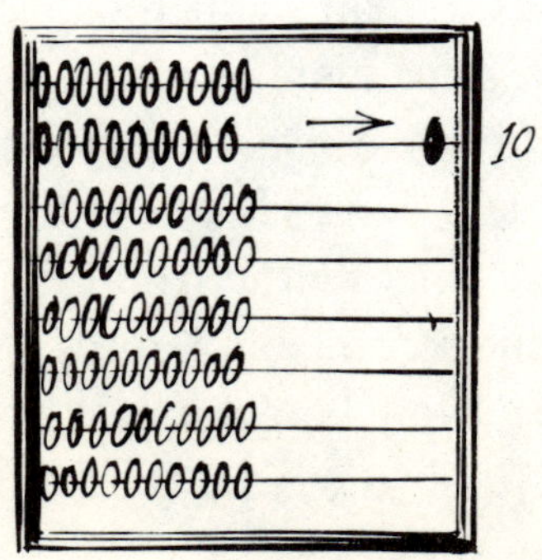

When all the first-row beads have been moved
again, he moves another second-row bead over to say
"twenty," and so on to "ninety-nine." After that he
moves a third-row bead over to say "one hundred,"
and all the beads on the first two rows go back to
the left to start over again.

Here's the way 174 looks on the abacus:

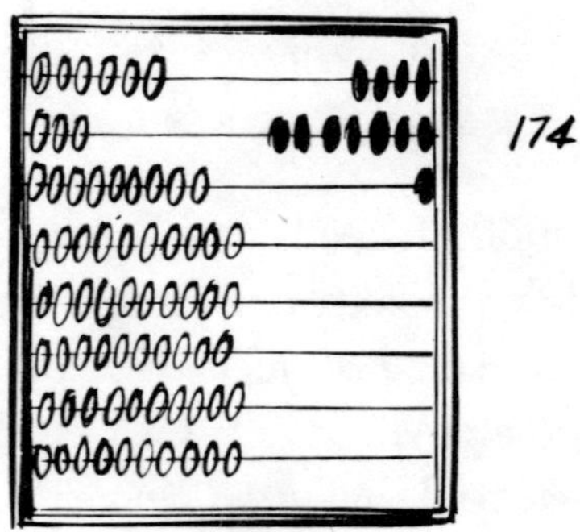

Suppose the old man wants to add 53 to that number. He moves three more beads on the first wire, and
then he should move five on the second. But there
are only three left there. He moves the three and then
"carries" by moving another third-row bead to stand
for all ten in the second and returns the entire second
row to the left. Now he can move two more second-
row beads to finish the 5 he is adding, which leaves
the abacus like this:

When he wants to subtract, he just counts off the beads backward, from right to left.

Actually, the old man is probably using an abacus that is divided in the middle with only seven beads on each wire, five on one side of the middle bar and two on the other. He counts the left beads and then "carries" five by moving *one* of the right beads on the same wire and returning the left five. The principle is the same: the abacus enables him to do arithmetic by counting.

Calculating machines work the same way. The first was invented in France by a nineteen-year-old mathematician named Blaise Pascal about the time the Pilgrims were having their first Thanksgiving over here.

Instead of beads, the machine used wheels that turned one notch for each number. When a wheel turned past nine, it hooked the wheel beside it and turned it one notch. Pascal had invented a mechanical abacus with an automatic "carry."

Another mathematician named Gottfried Leibnitz added some more gears and wheels so that Pascal's machine could multiply by adding the same number to itself over and over again rapidly and divide by repeated subtraction.

Important? Yes. Did it change the world? No. The machine just wasn't that much better. Three hundred years later a man operating a vastly improved adding machine, the kind used in modern offices today, raced a Japanese clerk doing the same calculations with an abacus—and the Japanese with the ancient abacus won.

The first real computer didn't change the world either. It was never built. It existed, in fantastic detail, in the mind of a grumpy English mathematics teacher named Charles Babbage around the time of our Civil War. He loved problems and puzzles, as do computer people today. He taught himself arithmetic, and when he went to college, he knew more algebra than his teacher. He invented speedometers and a machine for playing ticktacktoe. Later he built an adding machine that could solve a particular kind of problem. Then he began to design an "analytical engine" that could solve any kind of arithmetic problem.

In those days, rugs were woven on automatic looms controlled by paper cards. Holes in the cards allowed rods which were connected to different-colored threads to poke through. The pattern of holes in the cards controlled the pattern woven in the rug. To change the pattern, the operator just changed the cards.

Babbage put together the idea of instructions stored in punched cards with the idea of a calculating machine. To set up the machine to solve a new problem—weave a new arithmetic pattern—he would just change cards. The two ideas added up to a sum vastly greater than its parts. Inside Babbage's head was the first true computer.

His design was practical, but it required cogwheels and gears and other parts that the metalsmiths of his time could not make, and so the analytical engine had to wait a hundred years to be translated from a brilliant idea to a working machine.

But ideas are as real as machines. In the 1940's when Professor Howard Aiken was developing the first practical computer, he discovered Babbage's work. The ideas were so close to Aiken's that he felt he had received a personal message out of the past.

Professor Aiken was building a computer named Mark I. Instead of punched cards, Professor Aiken used rolls of punched paper to tell the machine what to do. Electricity turned the counterwheels, and eight hundred thousand switches, buttons, and other electrical parts filled a room three times as big as an ordinary living room. Mark I clicked and clucked like a ladies' knitting club, but it could rattle out three calculations a second.

One of its first jobs was to expose a military pipe dream. The United States was at war with Germany, Italy, and Japan. The Army learned that the Germans were making a terrible new weapon: an electric cannon. Would it work? Thousands of equations were fed to Mark I to find out. It clucked its way through them in a few days. The results showed that the electric cannon was impossible. The United States stopped worrying about it, while the Germans continued to waste their scientists' time trying to build it.

The United States was building new guns too, and testing new kinds of ammunition. How high to point the gun barrels to fire at targets miles away, at various distances and under various conditions, had to be calculated to construct detailed tables of instructions for aiming the guns. A special kind of computer had been built for this work. Instead of counting, like the abacus, it measured lengths.

By using proportionate lengths to represent quantities, this kind of computer makes a special model, or "analog," of the problem, and so it is called an "analog computer." The accuracy of the analog computer depends on how accurately the lengths can be measured. For example, the slide rule is a handy analog computer used for quick approximate answers. With practice on the slide rule you can read answers accurate to three or four decimal places.

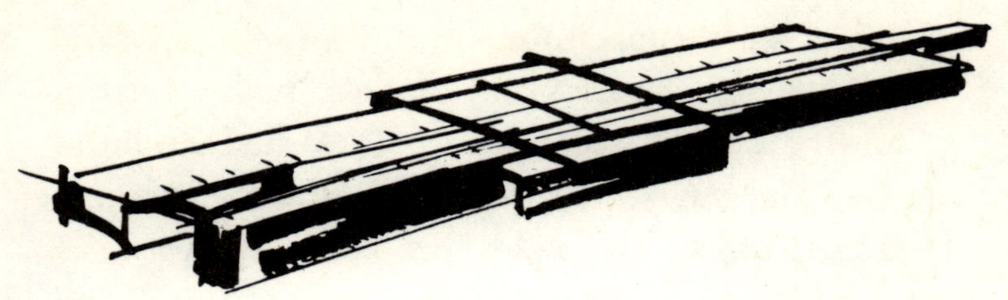

The gun tables required precise calculations, and a scientist named Dr. Vannevar Bush had built a huge analog computer to do them. The answers were expressed as lengths by the analog computer, and tiny but important differences were difficult to read.

The job required a digital computer to produce answers that didn't have to be measured. Mark I was accurate, but too slow. A problem went only as fast as its thousands of mechanical switches could open and close.

Everything was ready for the great invention: a digital computer fast enough to satisfy the urgent wartime need. Aiken had developed the basic design. All that remained was to find a switching device that could work faster than Mark I's mechanical insides.

The device was there too, waiting to be recognized. It had been around for years, not just in laboratories but in homes and automobiles too—inside the ordinary radio.

It was the vacuum tube.

Imagine an abacus made of light bulbs. Instead of moving a bead, switch on a bulb. When ten bulbs are on in a row, switch them off and switch on one bulb in the next row, and so on. Here's the way 174 would look:

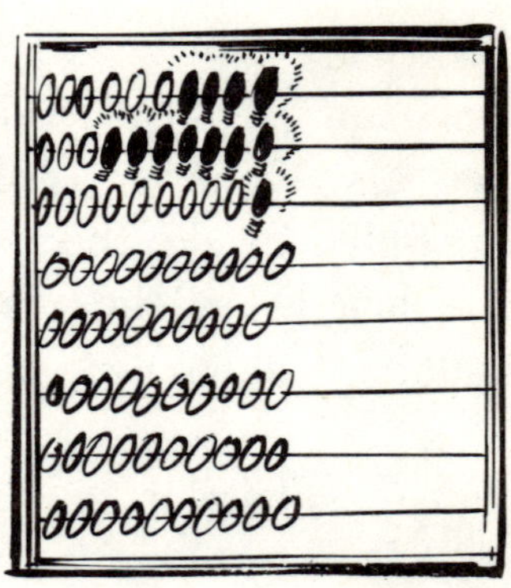

A vacuum tube looks like a skinny light bulb. Vacuum tubes can be connected as switches to control one another. With no mechanical parts involved, only the electricity moves to turn the tubes on and off. Because electricity moves so fast, the vacuum tube can turn the flow on and off in about one-millionth of a second.

When two scientists named Dr. Presper Eckert and Dr. John Mauchly used vacuum tubes instead of Mark I's mechanical switches, they invented the first electronic computer. Instead of three calculations a second, their computer could do five thousand.

They gave it an important-sounding name, the Electronic Numerical Integrator and Calculator, but then they used its initials as a nickname—ENIAC. Ever since, computer people have made up names with initials that spell nicknames, often with a smile behind them. SALE, for example, stands for Simple Algebraic Language for Engineers, and JOVIAL for Jules's Own Version of the International Algebraic Language.

But there was no smile behind the jobs the computer was given. In 1948, America's atomic-bomb research had one project that required nine million calculations. Fifteen hundred engineers would have had to work a year to solve them all. An electronic computer built by the International Business Machines company did the job in 150 hours.

Thinking about it later, Dr. Eckert wondered why the electronic computer had taken so long to be invented. "What puzzles me," he said, "is that there wasn't anything in the ENIAC in the way of components that wasn't available ten and possibly fifteen years before. . . . The real question is, why wasn't it done sooner?"

Dr. Mauchly answered, "In part, the demand wasn't there. The demand, of course, is a curious thing. People may need something without knowing that they need it."

Even Dr. Mauchly didn't realize how great was the need for the computer. In 1948, he thought five or six companies might use computers. Actually, within ten years there were over a thousand in use. Before another ten years had passed, there were fifty thousand, and the number was growing faster every year.

Old Babbage's idea had reached its time.

3
SWITCH ARITHMETIC

Computer people tell a riddle about an astronaut who
meets a creature on another planet. He can see that
the CAP (Creature on Another Planet—you'd better
get used to these nicknames) is carrying complicated
equipment, and it seems friendly. As the astronaut

tries to think what to do or say, the CAP draws in the dust with its tentacle:

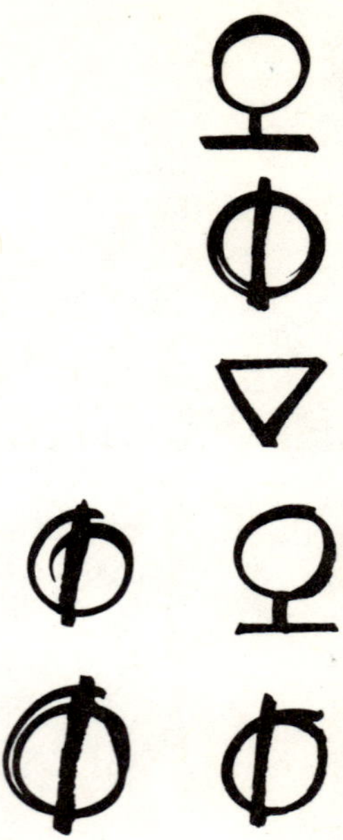

What does that mean?

As the astronaut studies the marks, he thinks: the CAP seems friendly, and so the marks are probably an attempt to communicate; they must represent an idea so basic the CAP believes any intelligent creature would recognize it; the complicated equipment must have been produced by some kind of science; perhaps the idea is basic to all science.

At that thought, the astronaut picks up a stone and marks alongside the symbols:

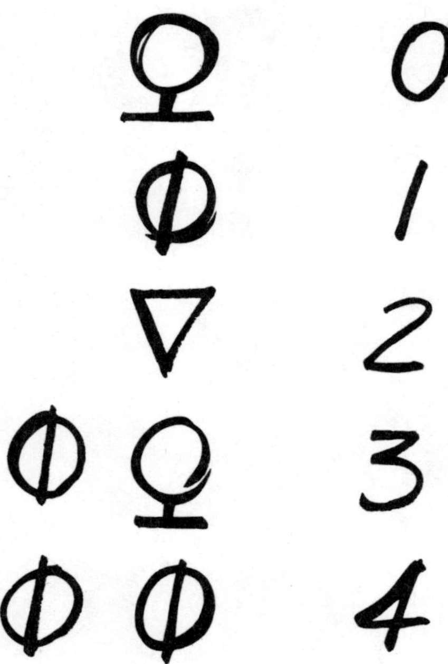

They are in communication.

The astronaut knew that arithmetic is the language of science, and all numbering systems use symbols to stand for quantities (ours uses 1, 2, 3, etc.; the Romans used I, V, C, M, etc.). How many symbols is not important. When we want to express a number bigger than our last symbol, we just start over again—10, 11, 12, or X, XI, XII, etc.

The astronaut realized the CAP used a three-symbol system:

and then started over again:

just as we do after ten symbols.

Any number of symbols more than one can be used in a numbering system. Two is the minimum because complicated problems require not just the idea of a quantity, but also the idea of zero. Obvious as it seems, this idea took hundreds of years to develop.

Roman numerals, for example, have no zero. Some unknown Hindu genius made what may be the most important discovery in mathematics: the discovery of nothing. He made a symbol called *sifr*, meaning empty, to stand for the unused row of beads on the abacus.

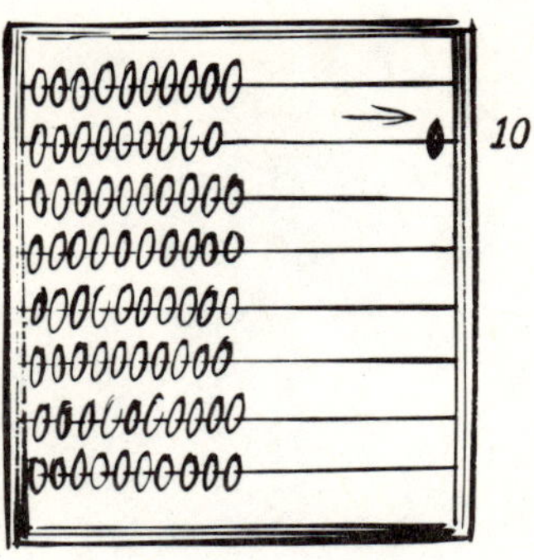

This word came to be called "cipher" and finally "zero."

Using just zero and one, counting looks like this:

0	0
1	1
2	10
3	11
4	100
5	101
6	110
7	111
8	1000
9	1001

It looks odd at first because a ten-symbol system is so familiar. But we got started with ten symbols just because we started counting on our fingers. Two-symbol arithmetic, which is called binary arithmetic, is really simpler. To learn "sums," for instance, you just have to remember three operations:

$$0 + 0 = 0$$
$$1 + 0 = 1$$
$$1 + 1 = 10$$

Try it:

```
    7=  111
+   6=  110
       ————
        001      first sum
        11       carries
   13=1101       final sum
```

With only 0 and 1 you have to use a lot of digits to express even small numbers, and so adding requires a lot of carrying to the left. But any addition can be done with just the two symbols by following the three simple operations.

Subtraction works almost the same way. First the digits of the number to be subtracted are reversed—all the ones are changed to zeros and the zeros to ones—and then the two numbers are added, following the same rules with one extra: the "one" that always comes up on the left is carried all the way back to the right and added to the one or zero in the first column:

$$
\begin{array}{rcl}
7 & = & 111 \\
-6 & & 001 \qquad \text{110 reversed} \\
\hline
& & 110 \qquad \text{first sum} \\
& & 1 \qquad \text{carry} \\
\hline
& & 100 \\
& & 1 \qquad \text{carry} \\
\hline
& & 1{,}000 \\
& & 1 \qquad \text{carry back} \\
\hline
1 & = & 001
\end{array}
$$

The rules of multiplication are as simple as those of addition:

$$
\begin{aligned}
0 \times 0 &= 0 \\
0 \times 1 &= 0 \\
1 \times 1 &= 1
\end{aligned}
$$

Here's the way 2×3 works:

$$
\begin{array}{rl}
3 = & 11 \\
\times\,2 = & \times\ 10 \\
\hline
& 00 \qquad 0 \times 1 = 0;\ 0 \times 1 = 0 \\
& 11 \qquad 1 \times 1 = 1;\ 1 \times 1 = 1 \\
\hline
6 = & 110
\end{array}
$$

Besides being simple, two-symbol arithmetic is natural to the computer for another reason: the computer counts on two fingers. It is made of parts that work like switches, either on or off. "On" can stand for one, "off" for zero. Telling the computer to add turns on circuits that control the switches according to the three rules of addition.

The switches are electronic, like vacuum tubes,

and so nothing moves inside them but the electricity. They switch on and off in a few billionths of a second, which means the computer can solve complex problems in fractions of a second.

It's hard to imagine anything that fast. Sound travels about 750 miles an hour. A spaceship going into orbit around the earth travels lots faster—about 27,500 miles an hour. At that speed, in a millionth of a second the spaceship travels less than half an inch.

4
INSIDE THE INPUT

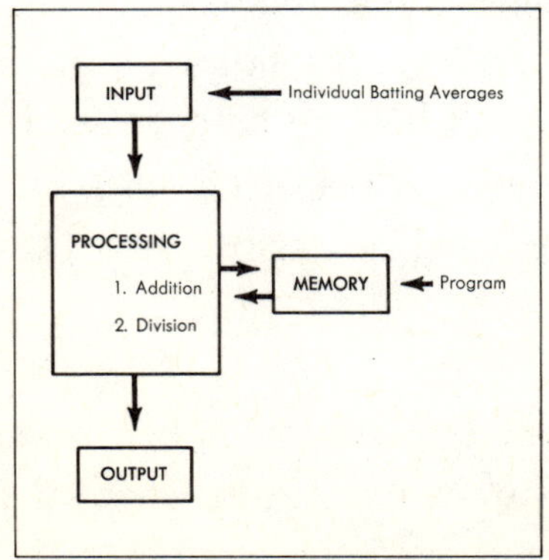

Remember the roadmap?

We've been inside PROCESSING, where we found a scramble of ones and zeros whipping through switches faster than spaceships. Before you could stop a "one" to look at it, it would be gone. It is only a tiny electric signal called a pulse.

When a pulse hits an "off" switch, the switch goes on $(1 + 0 = 1)$. When it hits an "on" switch, that one goes off and the switch next door goes on $(1 + 1 = 10)$, and so on. Numbers go through the computer as patterns of pulses. They start at the INPUT.

Indians sent messages by using a blanket to break a stream of smoke into puffs. To create a stream of electrical pulses, computers use punched cards like the ones that controlled looms in Babbage's time. There are two differences:

- Instead of rods with threads attached to them, brushlike wires connected to the inside of the computer poke through the holes.
- The cards don't have to be changed by hand. The operator loads a thick deck into the computer's card reader, and it snaps them through automatically.

As a hole goes by, the wire pokes through just long enough to touch an electrically charged roller, and—one!—a pulse goes into the computer.

Counting by punched cards started independently of the computer during the United States census of 1890. The previous census had taken seven years to finish. With some 12,000,000 more Americans to count, the census of 1890 wouldn't be finished in ten years—when the *next* census was due.

A statistician named Dr. Herman Hollerith invented a machine to read punched cards. With it, the job was done in one-third the time it would have taken and at five million dollars less than it would have cost.

The census takers' reports were coded and punched by hand into paper cards. Each card was put into a reader. Pins, like the rods of the automatic loom, dropped onto the card. Where there was a hole, the pin poked through and electricity clicked a pointer one place.

Years later Dr. Hollerith said, "As I recall it, I built only two of these machines and, instead of selling them or even renting them to the government, I ran them on the basis of so much per thousand cards sorted. It was a good-paying business."

His good-paying business grew into a whole industry employing hundreds of thousands of people and earning billions of dollars every year.

Today's punched card is a little bigger than a dollar bill. (It is actually the size of the old-fashioned dollar bill. One of the first International Business Machines factories was in Washington, D.C., where money is printed. Very good paper came cut into dollar-bill size, and the company bought the paper for punched cards.)

Instead of cards, some computers read punched paper tape. The principle is the same. A roll of tape is fed through a reader. Where there is a hole, an electrical pulse is created.

Of course, facts for input don't start out as holes in cards or paper but inside some human head. They have to go through trained fingers operating a keyboard like a typewriter's to get translated into punched holes.

Why not just send the signals from the fingers right into the computer? Because the computer is too expensive to slow down to finger speeds. Cards and tape can be punched while the computer is doing something else, and then they whip through the reader fast enough to send hundreds of pulses a second into the computer.

But the computer operates in billionths of a second, and so it still would have to spend most of its time waiting if the punched information were not changed again into a form that can be read a hundred times faster: tape coated with an iron compound. From punched holes, information is translated into invisible magnetic spots.

For some reason no one fully understands, when the tiny particles of certain metals are lined up facing the same way, they create a force called magnetism, which pulls at other pieces of the same kinds of metal. This pull is used to store information on the coated tape. The tape is moved past a tiny coil of wire. To record a "one," electricity is whirled through the coil. This pulls the atoms in the coating around to face a single direction, which makes a magnetic spot.

Whatever causes the atoms to line up along a flow of electricity works in reverse, too: once a spot has been magnetized on the tape, moving it past a coil of wire *causes* a flow of electricity in the coil. To read the information, the coded tape is pulled past the same tiny coils. Where there is a spot, a tiny current runs through the coil to tell the computer "one."

The same coil reads and writes hundreds of thousands of binary encoded numbers a second on the same magnetic tape without even touching it. A computer could read this whole book in less than a second if the letters were represented by numbers written on magnetic tape.

And this book *could* be written on magnetic tape. Suppose 0 stands for A, 1 for B, 10 for C, and so on. The word "and" would be 0 1101 11. The computer could read letters and words as easily as numbers and equations. Inside the computer they would "look" just alike, and so if someone made a mistake, the computer would make a mess trying to add and subtract words instead of numbers—which sometimes happens.

People occasionally have to stop the computer to correct a mistake, tell it what to do next, or give it new information. Then for a few minutes the computer slows down to our speed while an operator uses a special typewriter connected to the computer to send signals right into it. When he's finished, the computer types its "answers" back to the operator. When he presses a button on its blinking face, the computer goes back to full speed again.

Punched cards, too, are used to get information *from* the computer as well as to put it in. Not information for people to read—punched holes are slow reading even for computer people—but information for other machines to translate back into letters and numbers on paper. First the computer translates the numbers from its two-symbol system back into our ten-symbol system. Take a number: 148. The computer could punch one hole, then four, and then eight, which would look like this:

Actually, it just punches the last hole in each column, like this:

Then the cards are put in a printer, which reads just like a card reader—wires poke through the holes and touch a roller to complete an electrical circuit. But as the roller moves the card through the printer, a print wheel also moves in step with it.

When the wire pokes through the card, the printer gets a pulse that triggers the wheel to print.

Letters are coded with two punches in the same vertical row. The first is above the numbers.

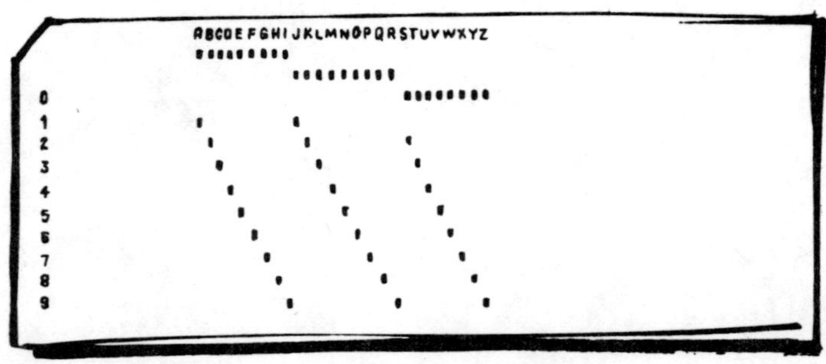

That pulse zips the print wheel around to the correct general section of the alphabet, and then the wheel just clicks along in step with the roller until it gets the next pulse that says "print."

There are other ways to put information into a computer and get answers from it. Some computers answer questions with a human voice. There are schoolrooms full of typewriters and television sets where students carry on separate "conversations" with the same computer all at the same time.

But first—have a look inside the MEMORY block.

5

REMEMBERING ONES AND ZEROS

Inside your head is a three-pound gray mass that has ten thousand times as many memory cells as the biggest computer. It uses pulses of electricity too, but one of the simplest things it does is remember. It also thinks, imagines, believes—even dreams.

All the computer's memory can do is store ones and zeros. It is made of doughnut-shaped magnets, called cores, not much bigger than a period on this page. Perhaps a million of these cores are threaded on thin wires crisscrossed like the strings of a tennis racket.

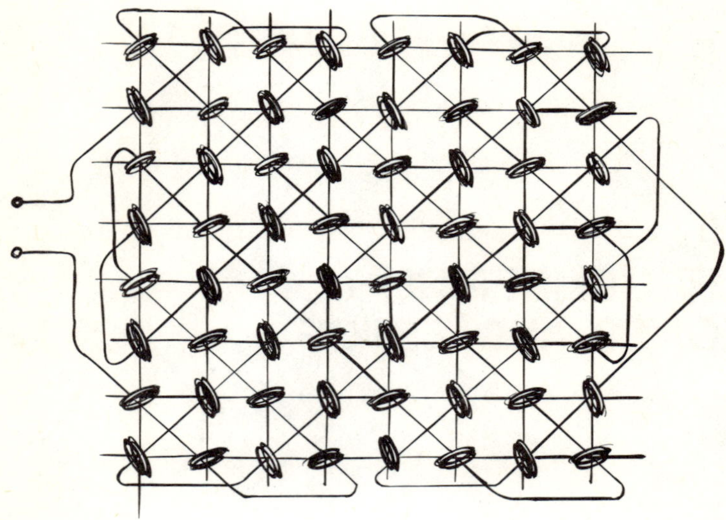

The "rackets" are wired together in stacks.

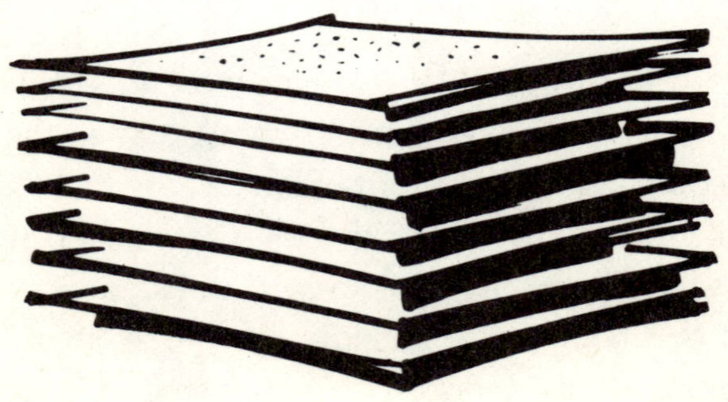

When electricity runs through a wire strung through a core, the molecules line up facing the same way in the core.

Suppose the core started out magnetized in this direction:

When the direction of the electricity is reversed, so is the magnetism in the core.

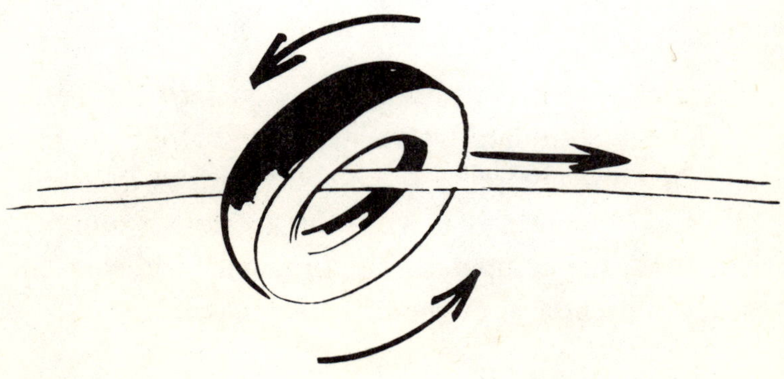

One of these directions represents a "one" and the other a "zero."

Here's the way nine looks in the memory of a computer:

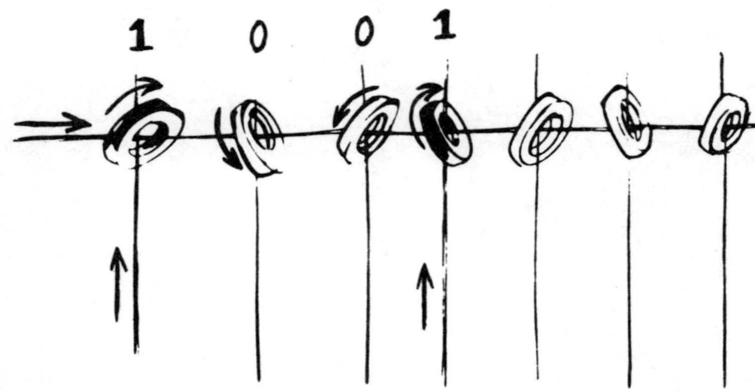

Remember that a pulse doesn't go *into* the core; it just goes through, which makes the atoms of the core line up. The pulse keeps going, and so it affects all cores strung on that wire. But to store a number like 1001, the computer must turn only one core on or off in each layer of the memory stack.

Notice that each core circles the place where two wires cross. This means that, although each goes through many cores, any *two* wires meet at only *one* core.

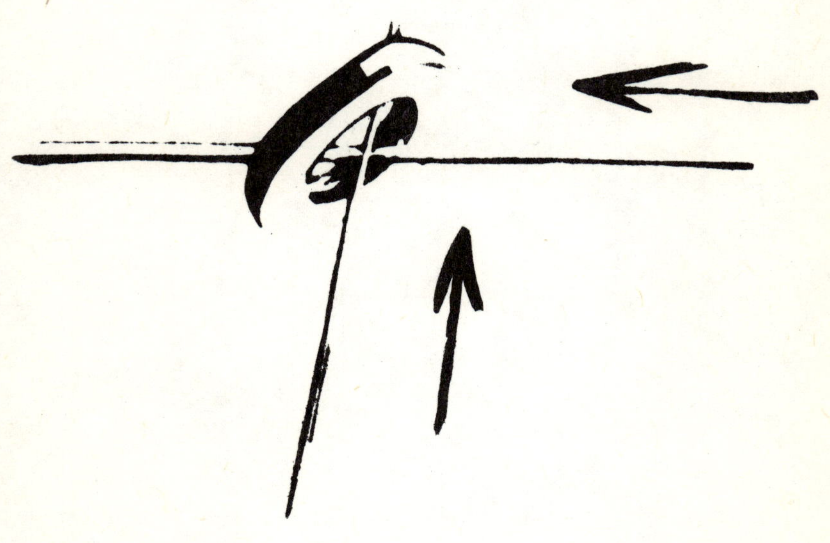

Instead of sending the pulse along one wire, which would affect all the cores on the wire, the input sends a half-size pulse along each of two wires. Only the

core where those two wires meet gets the full pulse,
and so only that core is turned on.

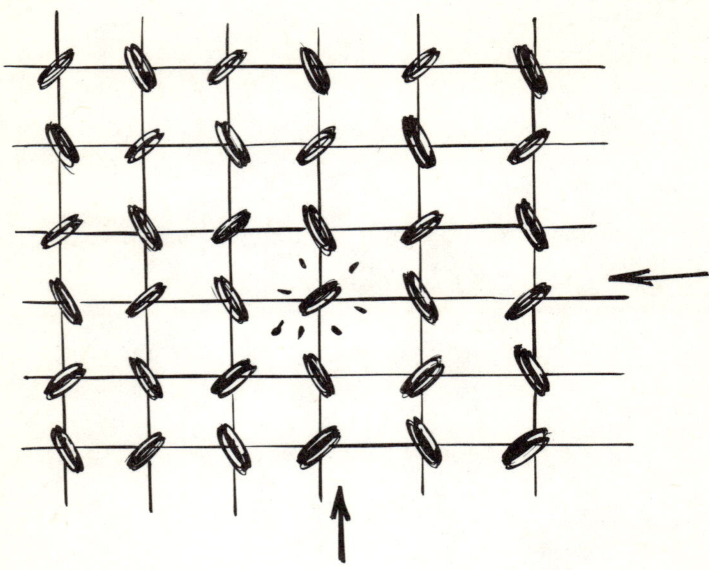

To do anything with that "one," the computer
must also be able to "read" it—to take it out of memory at the right time to use it in calculations.

Reading is very similar to storing. If a "one" is
stored in a core, the core is magnetized in the "one"
direction. If we try to store a "zero" in this core, the
magnetism reverses and this "switching" can be de-
tected by a third wire, called a sense winding, that is

laced through each one of the tiny cores. To read a core, the computer sends a half pulse through each of the first two wires, just as if it were storing a "zero." If the core is a "one," the atoms about-face, which sends a pulse through the third wire that says "one" to the computer.

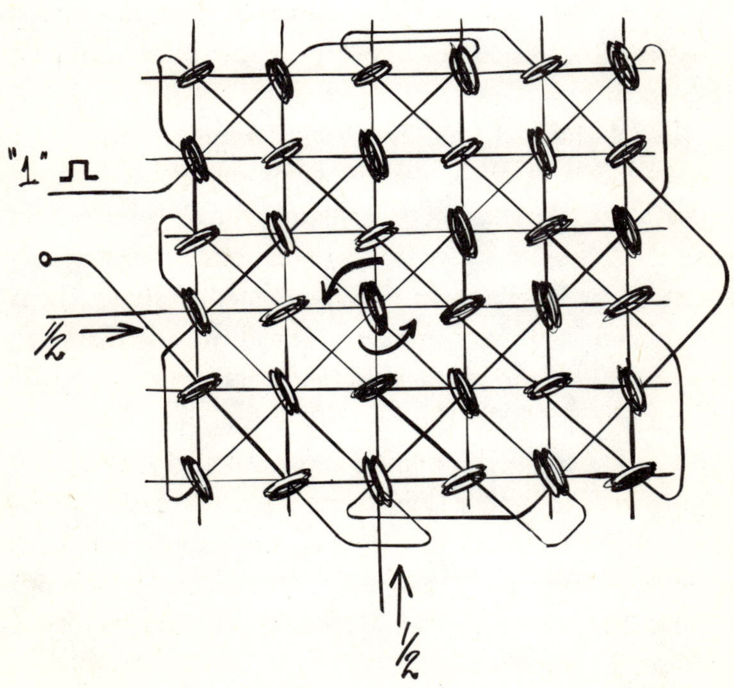

If the core is a "zero," the atoms don't change. No pulse goes through the third wire, and that says "zero."

Because reading involves writing a zero, the "one" core gets turned off just by reading it, and so the computer now has to send another pair of half pulses down the same wires in the other direction to turn it back on again.

Like everything a computer does, that seems a lot of trouble to do something simple—just store a "one" or a "zero." But since nothing moves but the electricity, the core is turned on or off in a few billionths of a second.

For additional memory, some computers use what looks like a stack of overgrown phonograph records, and others use big metal cans or drums. Information is stored the same way it is on magnetic tape, as a pattern of magnetic spots. Read-write coils above them are wired into the computer. The drums or disks are spun rapidly. As a magnetic spot goes past a coil, it sends a pulse into the computer that says "one."

Compared to the magnetic-core memory, the computer has to wait a long time—perhaps a few thousandths of a second—for the disk or drum to turn past the coil. But each magnetic spot doesn't have all those tiny wires threaded through it, and so drum and disk memory are not so costly to manufacture.

Some computers use all three kinds of memory: cores for information used all the time, drums for information used not so often, and disks for "reference book" information.

A special computer for an atomic-power laboratory in California has a trillion "ones" and "zeros" in memory. Suppose all that information were printed in a big book and you sat down to read it. You would finish in about two hundred years.

6

TELLING THE COMPUTER WHAT TO DO

What happens when you try to divide by zero?

When ENIAC, the first electronic computer, tried, it blew out several hundred tubes. It would still be blowing itself up trying to do the impossible if someone hadn't changed its instructions.

The computer has to be told *everything*. Computer people never think of it as an "electronic brain." Sometimes it seems more like a moron. Working with a computer is like sending a dull but obedient friend from house to house around your neighborhood to do something he cannot understand or even imagine:

"Go to the house 1221 and get the number waiting for you. Then go to 1446 and get the number there. Take them both over to the processor and tell it to add. Take the number that comes out up to the house at 2327 and leave it there, and then go to 1501 for your next instruction."

The "neighborhood" is the computer's memory, the tiny iron doughnuts or magnetic spots we saw in the last chapter.

Other machines remember too. A record player, for instance, remembers words and music stored on plastic disks. If it has a changer, the record player also follows instructions to go from record to record automatically.

But the record player does the same things to "Jingle Bells" that it does to "The Stars and Stripes Forever" or to a football fight song. Its instructions are not in its memory—the records—but in the machinery of its changer. The computer's instructions are stored in its memory.

That is an important difference. Groups of memory cores are numbered, just as the houses are numbered in your neighborhood, and so the computer can "travel" from address to address following one instruction and then finding the next.

"Go listen to Magnetic Tape Unit 12. Take the first number to address 1003. Then go get four words from the Card Reader. Put the first in address 2010, the second in 2020, the third in 2030, and the fourth in 2040. Then go to 1502 for your next instruction."

Because the computer travels around in its "neighborhood" just by turning magnets on and off, it can do complicated things very fast. It can figure out the instant to turn off a rocket engine on the way to the moon, the best mix of products for a chemical plant, or all the possible meanings for each word of an ancient manuscript written in a lost language.

What's more important, the same computer could do all those jobs, changing instructions from moon rocket to manuscript the way the record player changes from "Jingle Bells" to "The Stars and Stripes Forever."

The record player and even a washing machine can follow instructions, but a computer can also decide for itself *which* set of instructions to follow—if someone has told it when and how to decide.

Planning the approach to the job, setting the limits, defining the problems and exactly how they should be solved, step by step, are all done by people.

First they have to understand the job, which may take months of analysis. Then they lay out a general roadmap. Several other roadmaps of the same job, each more detailed, may be required. Then they write the individual instructions to the computer:

SELECT TAPE UNIT 200

READ RECORD INTO POSITIONS 1000 to 1050

ADD WHAT IS IN ADDRESS 184

The computer only works with ones and zeros, and so it can't obey the words ADD WHAT IS IN ADDRESS 184. Inside a computer, that instruction may look like: 000100000000000000000000010111000. Imagine writing a few thousand instructions like that!

Computer people don't have to. Instead they can instruct the computer almost the way they would talk to a dull but obedient friend:

READ INPUT TAPE 5

ADD DIVIDENDS TO INCOME

WRITE OUTPUT TAPE 6

GO TO 1

A set of instructions often ends on its way back to the beginning—"GO TO 1"—to start all over again. That's because the computer works so fast that hardly any job which only needs to be done once is worth the trouble of programming the computer.

Computers are used for jobs that have to be done over and over—jobs like figuring the earnings every week of each employee of a company, along with how much to keep back for his taxes, union dues, savings bonds, and contributions to charity. The last instruc-

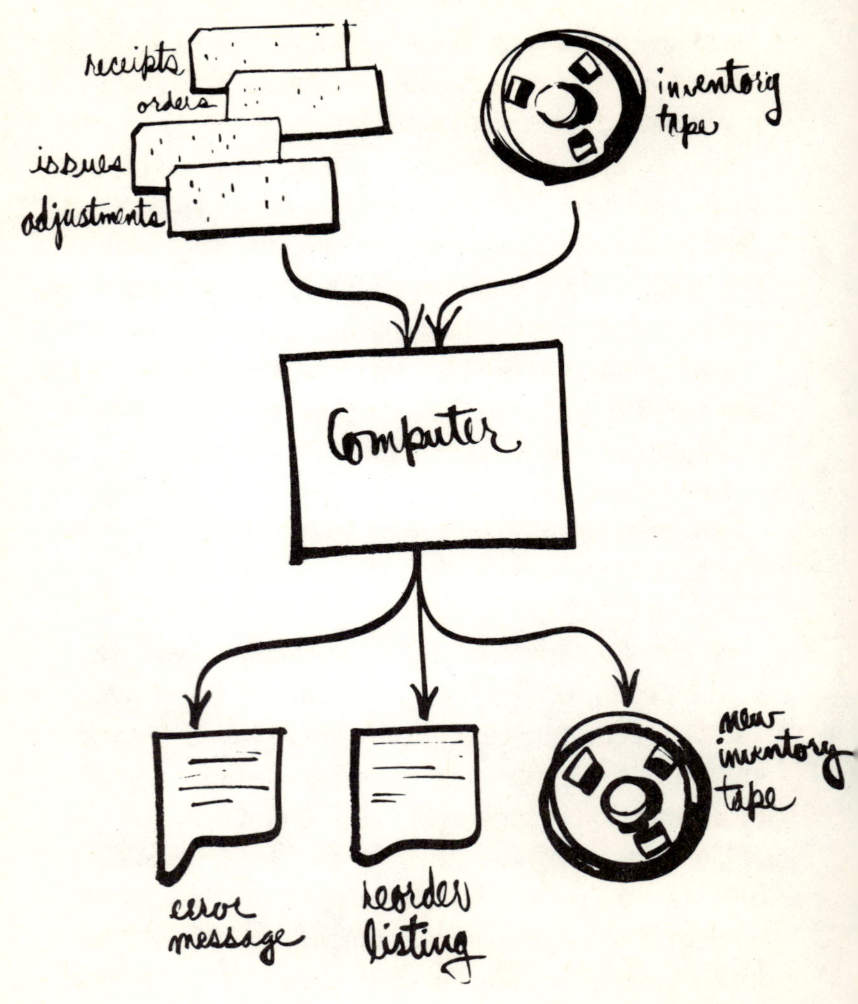

receipts
orders
issues
adjustments
inventory tape
Computer
error message
reorder listing
new inventory tape

tion tells the computer to start over again with another employee's earnings record. It goes through the same steps over and over until the last employee's paycheck is calculated. Then it stops and waits to be told what to do next.

When the programmer has written all the instructions for a job, ending with "GO TO 1" to tell the computer to start all over again, each instruction is punched into a card. Now the computer can read the instructions, but it still can't do what they say until each one is translated into the special code that matches the computer's circuits—for example, from ADD WHAT IS IN ADDRESS 184 to 0001000000000000-0000000000010111000.

To do this, before the program cards are fed into the computer, *another* set of instructions is stored in memory. This second set is a kind of computer dictionary that translates each of those dull-but-obedient-friend instructions into "ones" and "zeros."

One instruction like ADD DIVIDENDS TO INCOME requires several machine steps, each telling the computer with a code of "ones" and "zeros":

- WHAT to do—add, subtract, read a tape, etc.
- WHERE to go to get the information or put the results.

Using the computer dictionary, the computer can fill in all the detailed instructions—until someone makes a mistake and gives the computer an instruction that isn't in the dictionary. Even then the computer may be able to compare what it received with what is in the dictionary and then select a stored message phrase to send to the typewriter:

THE FOLLOWING FORMAT STATEMENTS HAVE

BEEN OMITTED . . . or

ILLEGAL USE OF PUNCTUATION . . . or

TOO MANY LEFT PARENTHESES

The first time I ever saw a computer, I was startled when the typewriter clattered away by itself. When I leaned over to see what it was writing, my neck prickled:

PAY ATTENTION TO WHAT YOU'RE DOING,

OR YOU'LL MESS UP THE WHOLE WORKS

AGAIN.

I looked up into the rows of switches and little flickering lights, and under the electric hum I heard a metallic chuckle.

It was just the sound of the card reader gulping a new deck of instructions, I learned later. And the message was a joke. Once an operator had put the wrong instruction cards into the computer, and so his friends on the night shift stored that "pay attention" message in memory, coded to come out to the typewriter when the card reader started.

ONE DAY IN THE MAXIPACK FACTORY

Suppose you and I own a factory that makes something called a "maxipack."

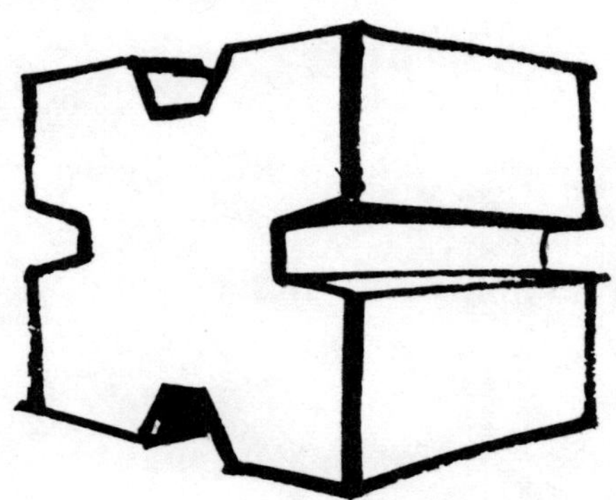

What does a maxipack do? Nothing. It's only as real as the factory we're supposing, but if you can suppose a factory, you can suppose a product for it too.

Inside each maxipack are two parts called "miniplexes":

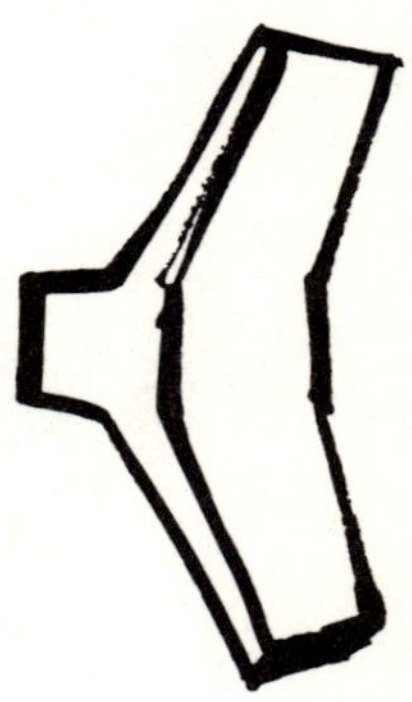

Suppose we buy the miniplexes from another company and then assemble them into maxipacks at our factory. We have some customers, some employees—and, of course, a computer.

To plan what we need to make the maxipacks our customers have ordered, we need to know:

- how many miniplexes are on hand, and
- how many are on order.

The sum of these is how many miniplexes we will

have available. We use the computer to keep track of this, and so we have stored the miniplex record on magnetic tape:

PART NUMBER	PART NAME	ON HAND	ON ORDER	AVAIL- ABLE	ORDER POINT	ORDER QUAN- TITY
123456789	miniplex	15	15	30	30	15

(The miniplex record also has the cost, name of the company that sells miniplexes to us, which of our other products use miniplexes, and a lot of other things—but forget about them for now.)

Watch what happens to that record during an ordinary day at the maxipack factory:

A new shipment arrives. The stock-room clerk unpacks the box, puts fifteen new miniplexes into the bin, and fills out a form called a receiving ticket to report that we now have more miniplexes on hand.

Later in the morning, while the clerk is unpacking a shipment of roller bearings, the supervisor of the maxipack assembly line asks for six miniplexes for that day's work. As the clerk counts them out of the bin, he notices that one of this morning's shipment is cracked. He keeps the supervisor waiting while he looks carefully at the rest of that shipment. Three others are broken.

After he has passed six good miniplexes across the counter to the supervisor, who grumbled all the time he was checking and then signing the issue slip, the clerk takes the four damaged miniplexes back to the shipping room to be returned to the supplier. He fills out an adjustment ticket.

While this has been going on, a girl in the Purchasing Department has been writing purchase orders for every part on a list printed by the computer. The number of miniplexes available—30—has gone to the order point—30—and so "miniplex" is on the list. She types a purchase order to the supplier for the order quantity—15.

A copy of that purchase order, along with all the others, goes to a key-punch operator. The stock-room clerk sends up the receiving tickets to her too. For each one she punches the part number and a code to tell the computer what kind of change this records— 1 for an order, 2 for a receipt, 3 for an issue, or 4 for an adjustment. Then she punches the number of parts involved.

For each form the key-punch operator punches a card that will tell the computer something that happened that day. Looking at the receiving ticket the stock-room clerk filled out after he put the fifteen new miniplexes into the bin, she first punches the miniplex part number, 123456789, which will say "miniplex" to the computer. Then she punches a 2, which is the code for "receipt." (It could be 1, or 43, or any number; at our factory, the code for a receipt happens to be 2.) Then she punches 15, to tell the computer how many miniplexes were received, and goes on to a new card for the adjustment ticket that records the return of the four broken miniplexes.

Again, 123456789 to say "miniplex," now a 4, our code for "return," and a 4 to tell the computer how many were returned.

Next a card coded 3 to tell the computer we used ("issued") some, and 6 to tell how many. Then a card to tell the computer we ordered 15 (code 1) .

Now the key-punch operator has translated every piece of paper recording what happened to the miniplex today into punched cards for the computer. But she is not thinking about miniplexes as she works.

As she works, she is wondering when the stock-room clerk is going to lunch today, hoping he might sit down at her table again, and when she punches the miniplex order card she makes a mistake: instead of one card, she punches two—both for a quantity of 15. Then all the cards are sent to the computer room.

The cards record all the changes, all the miniplexes and roller bearings and nuts and bolts and everything else that arrived or got used or ordered or returned that day. They are sorted by part number so that the miniplexes are not mixed up with the roller bearings or the nuts and bolts. Now the computer operator's job is

to put these changes into the record so that we'll
know how many of everything we have.

The computer operator finds a magnetic-tape reel
marked "Inventory Update Program," which is the
set of instructions that tells the computer how to
keep the record of all the parts in the stock room. He
puts the reel in a glass-faced tape unit and presses
the START key on the console.

The tape unwinds from the full reel onto an empty
one, whisking past a tiny coil of wire that reads the
magnetic spots and sends the instructions into the

computer's memory. When it comes to the end of
the program, the reel spins back the other way to re-
wind the tape.

While this is happening, the operator finds another reel marked "Inventory Master Record" and
puts it into another tape unit. This is the record of
how many of everything we had yesterday. Now he's
ready for today's changes. He stacks the cards from
the key-punch operator in the card reader. To write
the changes into the record, he presses START.

When the programmer wrote the instructions to
the computer for updating the inventory, he knew
the inventory master record would be stored on
magnetic tape, and so the first instruction in the program tells the computer to read a tape record. The
first record happens to be 123456789, *miniplex*. The
"Inventory Master Record" tape reel twitches, half
an inch of tape zips by the coil, and into memory
goes:

PART NUMBER	PART NAME	ON HAND	ON ORDER	AVAIL- ABLE	ORDER POINT	ORDER QUAN- TITY
123456789	miniplex	15	15	30	30	15

That is the way the miniplex record finished the
day yesterday. Now the computer is going to record
the changes that happened today.

The programmer also knew that changes in the inventory master record would be recorded in punched cards, and so the second instruction tells the computer to read a card, which happens to be "receipts." That goes into memory:

PART NUMBER	CARD CODE	QUANTITY
123456789	2 (which says "receipt" to the computer)	15

A shipment of roller bearings came in this morning, remember? This card could refer to that receipt, instead of the miniplexes. To be sure the computer is not about to add roller bearings or something else to the miniplex record, the next instruction tells it to put the part number from the master record into the adder, and the next tells it to subtract the part number that was punched in the card.

If the result is zero, the part numbers are the same, and so the computer will go on to enter the receipt. If the result is not zero, this receipt belongs to some other part number. In that case, the computer is instructed to make its own decision to go back to the first instruction: read another record from tape. It will keep reading tape records and subtracting the part numbers until it comes to a zero difference.

Other machines can also make a few simple decisions like that. A steam engine, for instance, may have a valve held closed by a spring.

When the pressure gets too high, it pushes the valve open and lets off some steam. You could say the steam engine had decided to blow off some of its own pressure.

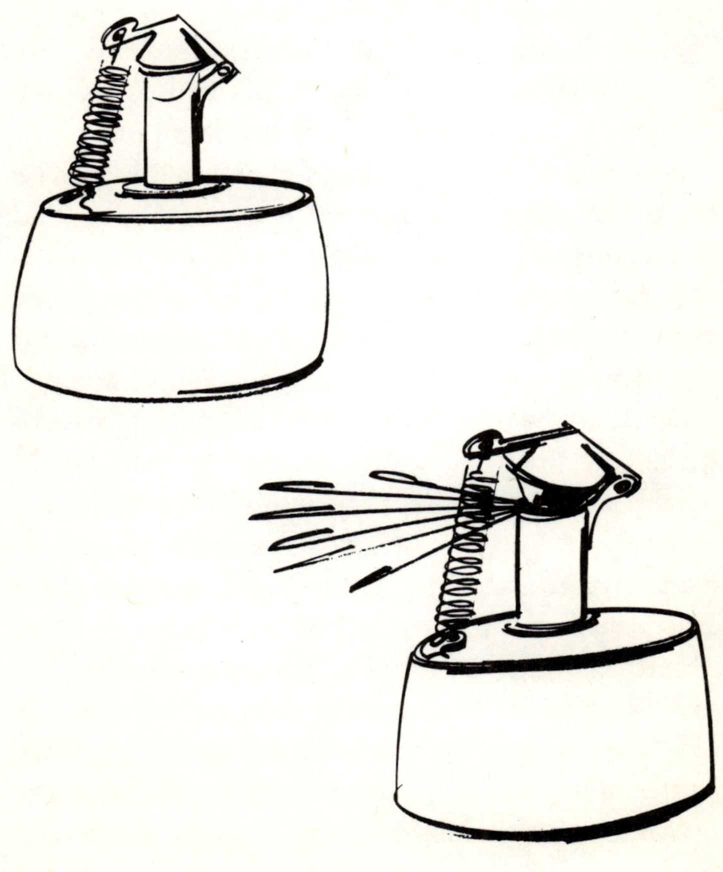

But the computer can make hundreds of decisions based on what happens as it goes along, so that it can do really complicated jobs. Watch how our maxi-pack-factory computer keeps making decisions just to keep track of one day's changes in the record of one part.

When it has decided that this is the miniplex receipt to match the miniplex record, the computer goes to the next instruction. That tells it to add three zeros to the card code, which makes it 2000, and then go to *that* address for its next instruction.

The programmer used the card code as the address key to the correct chain of instructions for each kind of card—receipts, issues, orders, etc. He did the thinking, but once the program is in the machine, the computer decides for itself which series of instructions to follow.

Address 2000 tells the computer to put the ON HAND quantity (15) in the adder, and then go to 2001.

2001: add the RECEIPTS quantity (15) and go on.

2002: put the sum (30) in the ON HAND part of the master record, which replaces the 15 that was there before this receipt.

2003: put the ON ORDER (15) in the adder.

2004: subtract the RECEIPTS (15).

2005: put the difference (0) back in the ON ORDER address (replacing 15), and then go back to the second instruction, which tells the computer to read a card.

The next card happens to be the "return" of the broken miniplexes. That goes into memory:

PART NUMBER	CARD CODE	QUANTITY
123456789	4	4

The third instruction tells the computer to subtract the part number from the one in the master record (remember?). The difference is zero again, and so the computer goes on to add the three zeros to the card code (4000) and then goes to that address for its next instruction. The programmer has stored a different series of steps beginning there to subtract the QUANTITY (4) from the ON HAND and AVAILABLE. Then the computer goes back to read another card, which happens to be the "order."

It checks stock number again and then goes to address 1000, where the instructions tell it to add the QUANTITY (15) to the ON ORDER and AVAILABLE, which, in our factory, means how many *will be* available, and so it is the sum of ON ORDER and ON HAND.

The roadmap for all that looks like:

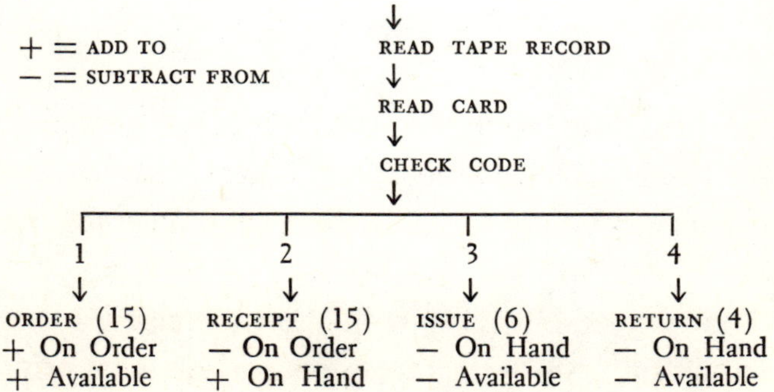

Here is the way all those pluses and minuses have changed the record:

PART NUMBER	NAME	TRANS-ACTION	ON HAND	ON ORDER	AVAIL-ABLE	ORDER POINT	ORDER QUAN-TITY
123456789	miniplex	beginning	15	15	30	30	15
		receipt	+15	−15			
		return	− 4		− 4		
		issue	− 6		− 6		
		order		+15	+15		
		end	20	15	35		

Remember the key-punch operator's error? Here comes another "order" card for 15 miniplexes. The part number checks zero, and so our dull but obedient friend adds three zeros to the card code and then goes through all the steps for an order again, adding 15 to ON ORDER and to AVAILABLE, which leaves the miniplex record like this:

PART NUMBER	NAME	TRANS-ACTION	ON HAND	ON ORDER	AVAIL-ABLE	ORDER POINT	ORDER QUAN-TITY
123456789	miniplex	end	20	15	35	30	15
		duplicate order		+15	+15		
		new end		30	50		

But the programmer knew that people make mistakes, and so he added some other steps to check every record before it got written back onto magnetic tape.

First, remember the girl in the Purchasing Department writing new orders for every part on a list printed by the computer? The parts got on the list when their AVAILABLE dropped to the ORDER POINT. Each part has its own order point, depending on how fast we use that part and how long we have to wait for a new shipment from our supplier.

The programmer knew that:

- a new order is never issued until AVAILABLE drops to ORDER POINT; therefore, the highest AVAILABLE can ever go is just after it has dropped exactly to the ORDER POINT and a new order has just gone out;
- a new order is always for the ORDER QUANTITY;
- therefore, any AVAILABLE higher than the sum of the ORDER POINT plus the ORDER QUANTITY must be a mistake.

And so the programmer added these instructions:

Put ORDER POINT into adder
↓
Add ORDER QUANTITY
↓
Subtract AVAILABLE
↓
Is the difference positive → YES → go on to
the next
instruction

↓
NO
↓
Print the record on the typewriter
as an error.

For the miniplex, the ORDER POINT was 30, the ORDER QUANTITY 15, but the AVAILABLE was 50—more than the sum—and so the computer caught the error and printed the record on the typewriter to be corrected.

The roadmap of all that looks like:

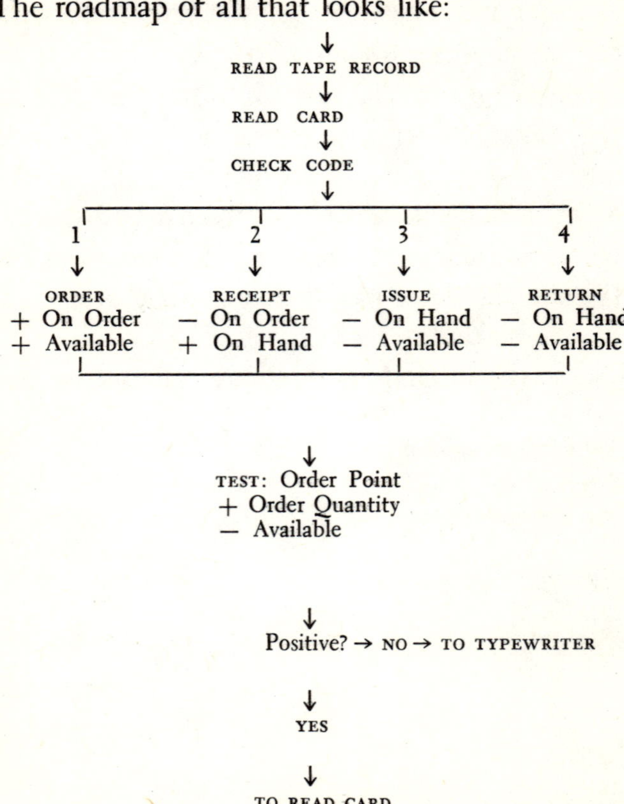

Notice the decision points:

· check card code

· test ORDER POINT

The programmer told it how, but the computer is deciding which logical steps to follow based on what has happened inside it in each case.

Old Babbage designed his analytical engine to be able to make that kind of decision too. He called it "the Engine moving forward by eating its own tail."

8
SPACESHIPS, SCHOOLROOMS, AND WRONG NUMBERS

While all this is going on at the factory, over at the lab an engineer is designing a new maxipack for next year's product line. He wants it to look like this:

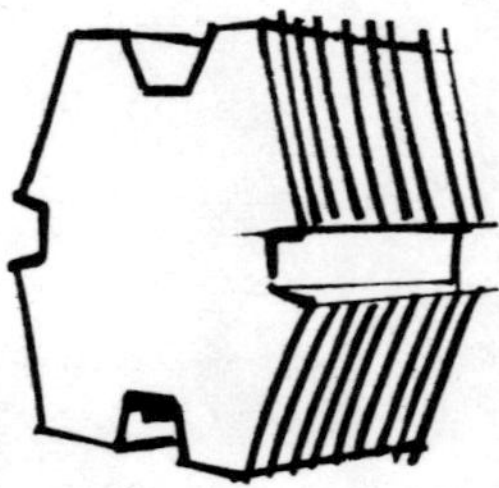

Will two miniplexes fit into that shape?

In front of him is a TV screen with a typewriter keyboard below it. He touches several keys, and a miniplex appears on the screen.

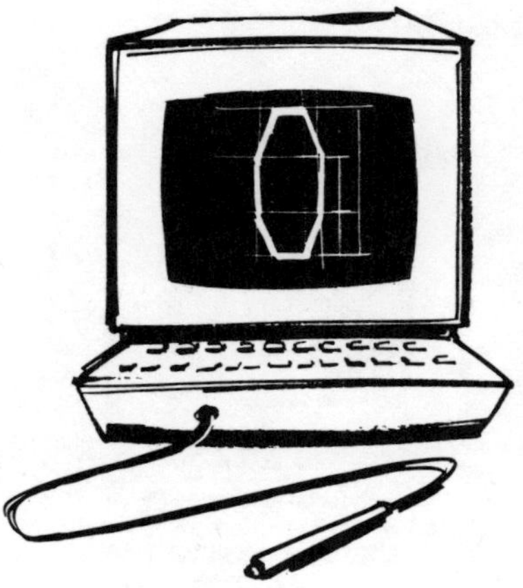

Using a special pen, which is wired to the keyboard, he sketches his new maxipack right on the screen. What he has sketched appears as an outline of light.

No problem that way—today's miniplex is neither too tall nor too wide for the streamlined style of his new design. He touches some other keys, the screen flickers, his sketch is gone, and the miniplex seems to twist around a little.

Another flicker, and it twists some more.

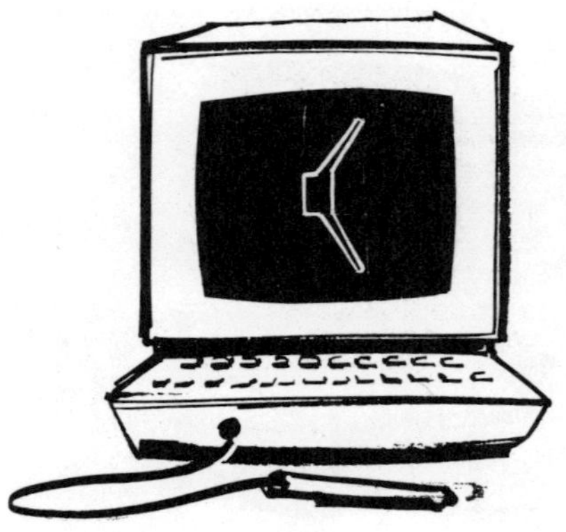

Again, and each flicker gives him a slightly different view, until the miniplex has turned all the way around to the side. Now he can see that it is too fat to fit into the new shape he has created.

What if he straightened those arms? He picks up the light pen, draws the new shape, and touches the key to turn the miniplex back around to see the front view.

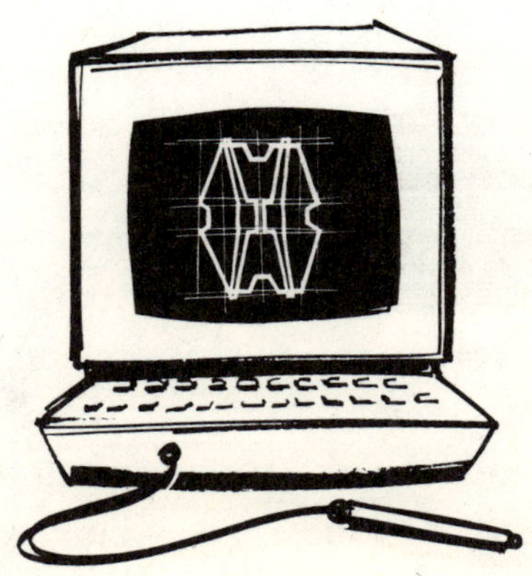

Now the arms stick up too high. He touches a key and erases his sketch. Another idea. He picks up the light pen and draws a new shape on the screen.

Behind the glass are hundreds of spots, each connected to the computer. Stored in the computer's memory is the pattern of spots that makes the shape of the miniplex.

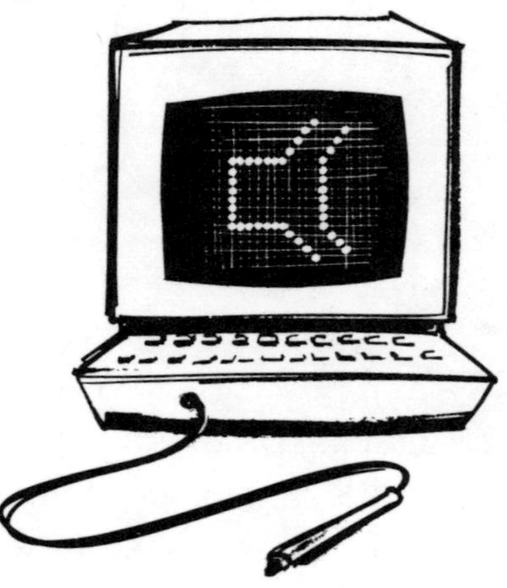

When the engineer keys the code that asks for the miniplex drawing, the computer "turns on" that pattern of spots. It draws straight lines between them, but the spots are so close together the lines seem to be smooth curves. When the engineer draws a new line, the light pen is actually sending pulses back into the computer to change the pattern.

With the computer, he has a kind of electronic blackboard—and much more. All the dimensions and other facts about the miniplex (and all the other parts of all the other products we make) are also stored in the computer's memory. When he finds a design change that looks right, the computer can immediately figure the effect of that change on the other parts and on the total product—how changing the miniplex's arms would change the size, weight, cost, and other characteristics of the maxipack.

The computer does all that in its spare time, while keeping track of parts and people and payments over in the factory. When the engineer keys a command, the computer finishes what it is doing—perhaps making all the changes to the miniplex record—and then in the half second while the tape unit is spinning to the next record, the computer changes the engineer's screen. It all happens so fast the operator never knows when the computer was interrupted, and the engineer, although he knows better, thinks of the machine as if it were his private answer box, just waiting for his next question.

Not just in our maxipack factory but everywhere, most computers spend most of their time keeping track of things. Money, for instance: how much is in the bank, how much each employee has earned, how much each customer owes us, how much we owe each supplier, and so on. The computer keeps track of money the same way it keeps track of miniplexes:
- read a change (such as a bill from a supplier);
- read a record (what we owe that supplier);
- compare identification numbers—if they don't match, read another record;

- when they match, process the change (add the amount of this bill to the total we owe that supplier) ;
- test: is the result unreasonable (is the new total higher than what we usually buy in a month from that supplier) ?
- if yes, print the record on the typewriter for examination;
- if no, write the changed record on magnetic tape.

But anything, such as the electronic blackboard, that can be a pattern of on's and off's can be manipulated in the computer—so fast the answers seem to be instantaneous.

Radar signals bounce off a spacecraft back to computers on earth. By complex mathematics, several "sightings" are combined to find where the spacecraft is. Several of those positions are combined to find where it is going. In a couple of seconds, the computers predict exactly where the spacecraft will be at any moment during the next eighteen hours.

Another special computer is inside the rocket itself. Instead of getting pulses from punched cards, the rocket computer gets pulses from instruments that measure how fast the rocket is going, in what direction, how much fuel is left, and dozens of other facts. Inside its memory is stored what the instruments should say at every moment of flight, along with what to do if one of the readings begins to go wrong.

It watches the temperatures and pressures inside the

pipes and tanks and adjusts the valves that control
the flow of fuel. If, for instance, one of the engines
doesn't start, the computer opens a valve that lets
more fuel into the other engines to keep the rocket
on course.

How? By doing what a digital computer does—
turning switches on and off. Instead of, say, switching
on the tape drive to read a record, it switches on a
little electric motor connected to the fuel valve:

- read a gauge;
- compare what it says with what it should say;
- test: is the difference zero?
- if yes, read another gauge;
- if no, switch on a motor that opens or closes a
  valve.

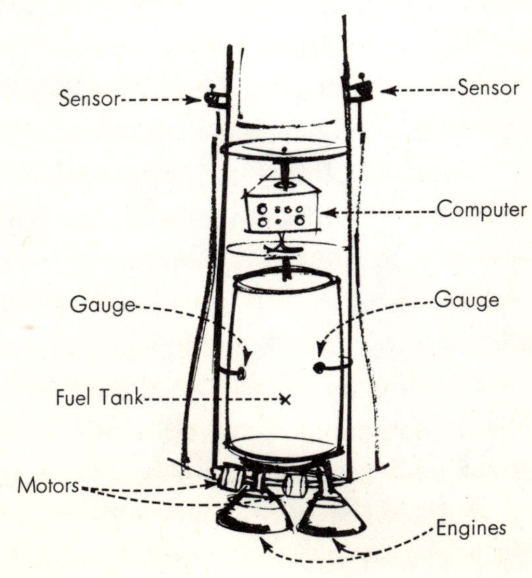

Not much different from what the computer does in the maxipack factory, but the difference is important. Instead of giving answers to people, the rocket computer is controlling a process *while it happens*. In the same way, earthbound computers control processes in steel mills, chemical plants, power generators, and in textile mills, where the punched-card-controlled loom started the process-control idea two hundred years ago.

Now the computer is reaching beyond the factory to touch the human life process. Some hospital patients are "wired" to computers that watch their breathing, heartbeat, temperature, and other processes, constantly comparing what is happening with what should be happening, just as the rocket computer does. When something begins to go wrong, the computer switches on a warning to the nurse.

The computer could switch on a record of the doctor's voice saying, "The patient in room 201 needs attention." To warn the nurse, a light that goes on under number 201 works just as well, but connecting a computer to a recording of a human voice is better for some other jobs.

Consider a problem of the telephone company: the day a new directory is published, it is already out of date. Every day people move into and out of town, and they get new telephone numbers.

Today their old numbers are connected to the operator's line, and their new and old numbers are stored together in a computer. When you dial a number that has been changed, an operator answers, "What number are you calling, please?" When you tell her the number, she taps it into a keyboard that sends it to a computer, which looks up the *new* number in its memory.

Suppose the new number is 656-5670. The computer *could* type that at the operator's terminal, and then she *could* tell you, "That number has been changed to 656-5670."

But instead, the computer goes to a special record player where, in a girl's voice, all the numbers have been recorded individually, "one, two, three, etc.," along with some sentences such as, "That is a working number. Please try it again."

In this case, the program sends the computer first to the place where "That number has been changed to . . ." is recorded. Then it goes to the place where the single word "six" is recorded, then to "five," back to "six," and so on to "zero."

You hear, "That number has been changed to six five six, five six seven zero." Each word is connected so quickly to the next they all sound like a single smooth sentence spoken with one breath. You may suppose you are still hearing the operator, who now is probably asking some other caller, "What number are you calling, please?"

Connecting a computer to a recorded human voice enables it to "talk" to anyone. Schoolchildren, for instance. Imagine a program for a third-grade mathematics drill. The instructions are recorded in a teacher's voice in the "record player," along with some special sentences such as:

"Add or subtract? Watch the signs."

"No, try again."

"Very good."

"Time is up."

and so on.

Now put an eight-year-old at a keyboard connected to the computer. On his head are earphones. He hears the teacher give him a problem: "Fourteen, take away seven."

He touches the "2" and the "1" keys. He hears, "Add or subtract? Watch the signs."

Now he touches the "7" and hears, "Very good," and gets the next problem.

A hard way to teach a little boy arithmetic? Yes, but doing anything once in a computer is the hard way. Hundreds of third graders can talk to the same computer all at the same time, and it answers so fast each one seems to have his own machine with a patient, friendly voice.

With a different program and a different set of recorded phrases, the computer can teach French or spelling or the facts of American history.

It can teach the facts, but not the meanings. The value of the computer in the classroom is the same as it is in the factory or during a space mission: the computer can deal with the routine facts faster and more accurately, leaving the people free to interpret the meanings.

9
ARTIFICIAL EXPERIENCE

A tree stump is a wooden model of the weather. The tree grew more in wet years than it did in dry ones, and every year's growth shows as a ring in the trunk—fat rings for wet years, skinny rings for dry ones.

Standing in the woods, you can see the sun and the clouds and the raindrops shining on the leaves, but looking down at the tree stump, you can see the weather.

In the same way, looking at the miniplex stock record, you can see the inventory.

PART NUMBER	NAME	TRANS-ACTION	ON HAND	ON ORDER	AVAIL-ABLE	ORDER POINT	ORDER QUAN-TITY
123456789	miniplex	beginning	15	15	30	30	15
		receipt	+15	−15			
		return	− 4		− 4		
		issue	− 6		− 6		
		order		+15	+15		
		end	20	15	35		

That list of numbers doesn't look like a miniplex any more than the growth rings in a tree trunk look like rain. But if you know the code, such as fat rings mean wet years and skinny ones dry years, you can see more in the model than you could standing in the woods—or in the maxipack factory stock room. In the stock room, you can see the 20 miniplexes on hand, but in the record you can also see the 15 that came in this morning, the four that were damaged and returned, the 6 that were given to the supervisor, and so on.

Of course, the inventory model doesn't show us the shape and size of the miniplex any more than the tree stump shows us the rainbows and the lightning flashes. The model shows only a simplified, special view of the real thing, but if you are interested in how many miniplexes are available for next week's work in the factory, the model's special view shows what you need to see.

The tree stump is a wooden model, and the stock record is a mathematical one. Both are historical models: they show what *has* happened.

After he was satisfied with the way it looked on the screen, the engineer we saw designing a new maxi-pack shape would probably make a *working* model of his new idea. It would be the new shape, perhaps bigger and cut open in front so that he could study the way the miniplexes work inside.

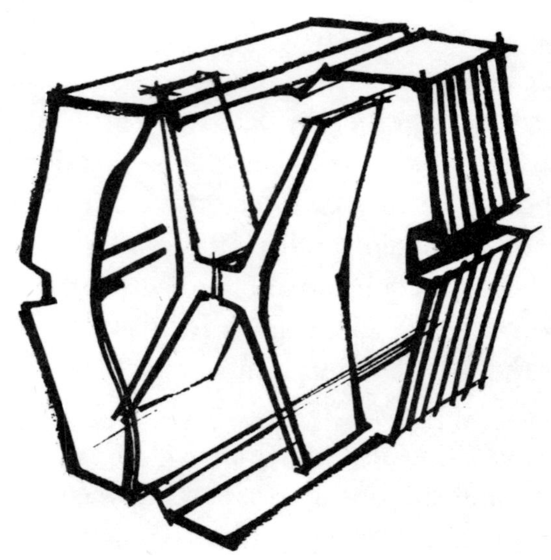

Some mathematical models also work.

Suppose the grouchy supervisor complained that sometimes there aren't enough miniplexes in stock, and so, while the engineer is changing the shape of the maxipack, you decide to change the order point of the miniplex.

Instead of 30, you decide to try 35.

Using the stock record as a working model, you try that order point to see what would have happened today. Instead of ending

ON HAND	ON ORDER	AVAIL-ABLE	ORDER POINT	ORDER QUAN-TITY
20	15	35	30	15

with an order point of 35, we would order another 15, bringing the record to:

ON HAND	ON ORDER	AVAIL-ABLE	ORDER POINT	ORDER QUAN-TITY
20	30	50	35	15

But suppose the bin holds only 35 miniplexes. If those 30 arrive on top of the 20 already on hand, there wouldn't be room in the bin. What is the right order point?

One day's stock record won't show us, but suppose you took three months' stock record as the mathematical model. Now you could keep trying different order points, working out what would have happened every day to create three months of artificial experience with each order point. If the past three months were not much different from what is coming up in the future, the artificial experience would show what you could expect with each order point.

Of course, by the time you finish all that arithmetic you might be *living* in the future you were trying to predict—but you wouldn't bother doing the actual arithmetic.

The computer can create three months' experience with 35 as the order point in a couple of seconds. Then it can test to see if ON HAND ever dropped to zero. If not, the supervisor would have always found enough miniplexes on hand. The computer could also test to see if there would ever be too many for the bin. If so, it could try another order point—28, perhaps—create three months' experience with that, test for zero and then for 35, and so on, until it found the order point that would keep enough on hand without overflowing the bin.

Inside the computer, the same simple things are going on—adding, going from instruction to instruction in memory, and testing the difference between plus, minus, and zero. The computer is answering questions planned by the programmer in advance. The difference is the *kind* of questions.

When the boy in the stock room opened the box

of miniplexes and filled out a ticket that went to a keypunch girl who punched a card that went into the computer, the computer changed a record to answer the question "What happened?"

When one of the rocket engines did not start, the computer compared what the instruments were telling it with what had been stored in its memory to answer the question "What *is* happening?"

When the computer creates artificial experience with different order points, it is answering the question "What if?"

Remember the streamlined maxipack our engineer designed on a TV screen connected to the computer? Suppose we find it would cost more to make, but that we can probably also sell it to some customers at a higher price.

Now we need two kinds of maxipacks, a streamliner and a "plainjane" economy model. Each uses the same number of miniplexes, but the streamlined maxipack takes longer to put together, uses a new colored plastic so that only the trim must be painted, but needs a second look on the way out of the plant to be sure any customer who pays extra for a streamlined maxipack is getting a perfect one.

To find how many of each of the two styles of maxipacks we could make in a week, we can draw a model of straight lines, called a *linear model*.

Suppose we find that five men on the assembly line now can put together ten plainjanes a week, but they could only assemble half as many streamliners. Count ten spaces along one line, call that "plain-jane"; five spaces along another, call that "stream-liner"; and draw a straight line called "assembly" between the two.

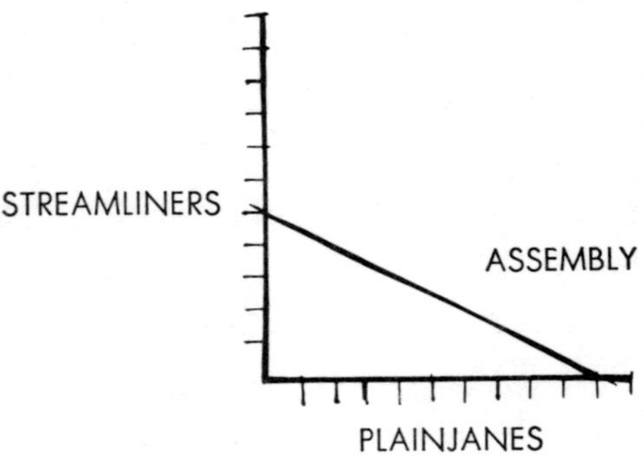

Inspection is a surprise. We are now checking five plainjanes a week; the streamliners are easier to see inside, and so we could inspect ten of them a week—and give them all a second look too, just to be sure.

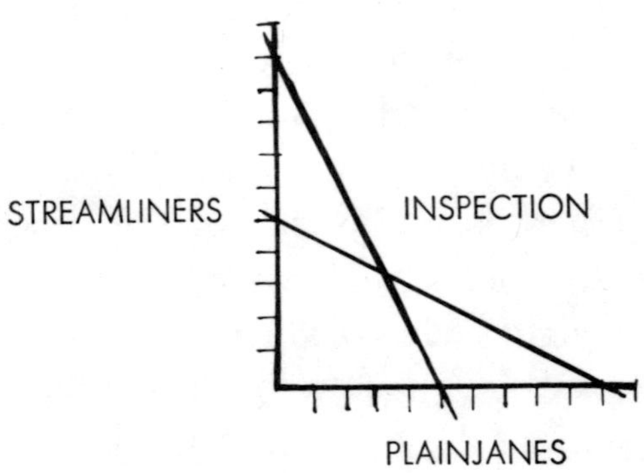

The paint shop can now spray ten plainjanes, base coat and trim, in a week. Using the new colored plastic for the base color, the streamliner only needs its trim painted—but it has more trim to cover. The paint foreman says he could handle seven a week.

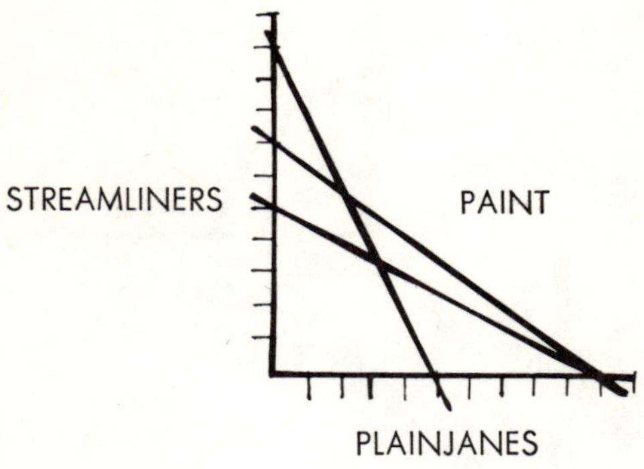

All the possible combinations of plainjanes and streamliner maxipacks we could make in a week are now on the left side of all three lines.

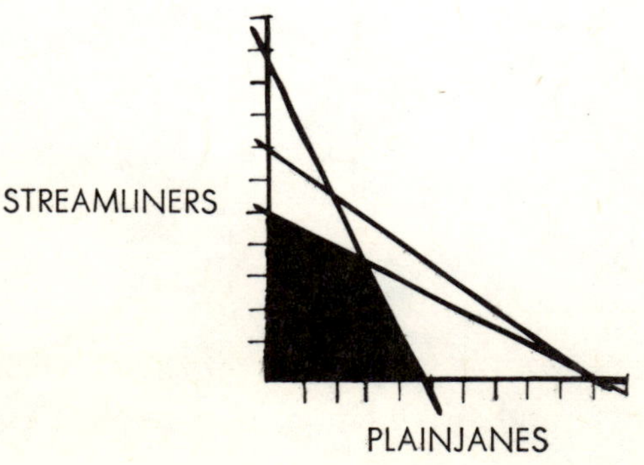

For instance, we could make three plainjanes and two streamliners,

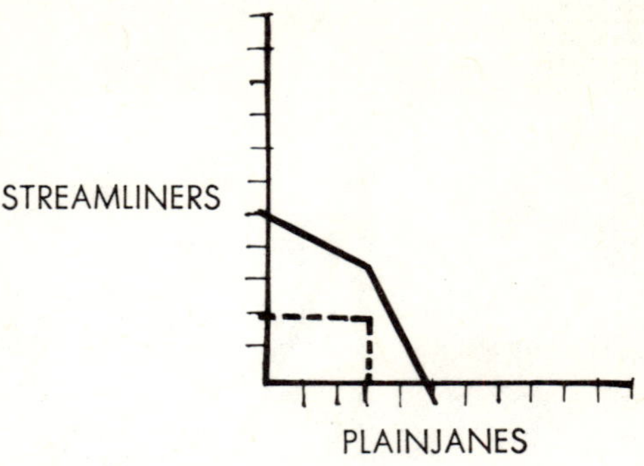

or five plainjanes and no streamliners, or one plainjane and four streamliners.

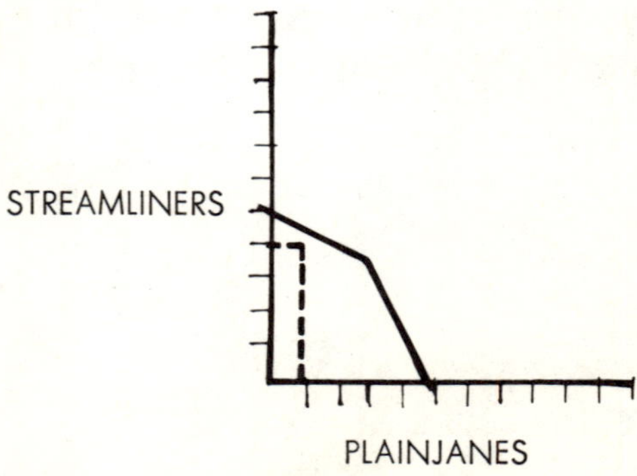

But suppose our sales manager says he can sell five streamliners and two plainjanes a week. Do we need to hire more assemblymen, more inspectors, or more painters?

The painting line is already outside the limits set by assembly and inspection, and so more painters can't increase production. If we added an inspector, our experience tells us that the line would jump to:

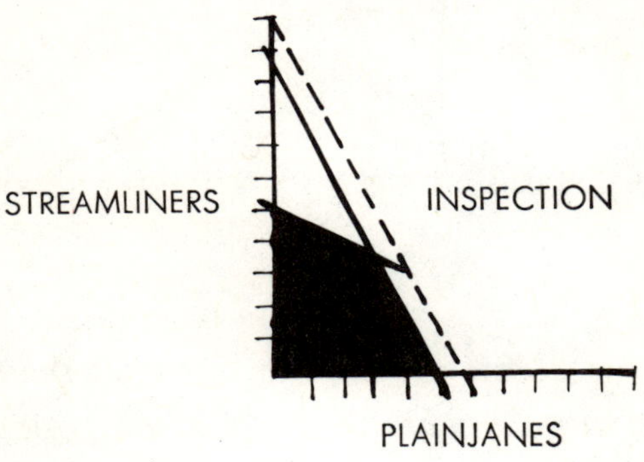

But the combination of five streamliners and two plainjanes still falls outside the boundary.

One more assemblyman would move that line to:

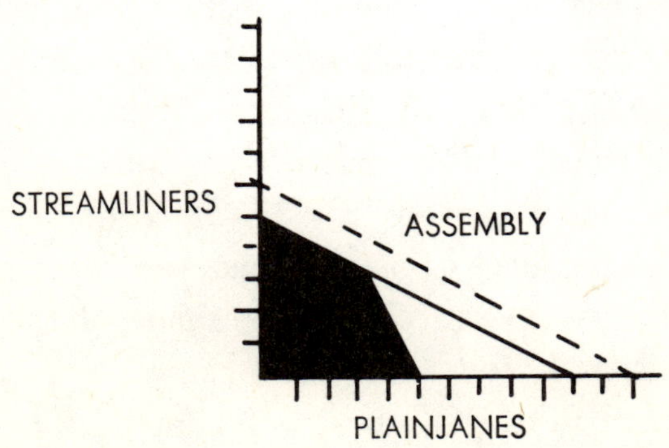

which would allow us to make what we can sell:

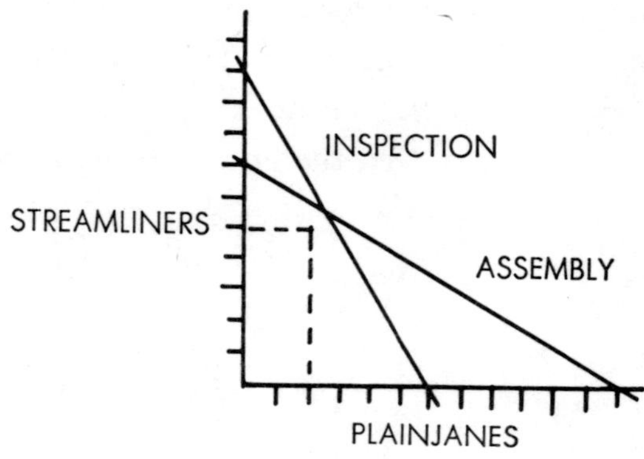

Before we decide finally, our linear model will get
more lines to show what happens to our costs, profits,
floor space in the factory, and so on. Computing the
best product mix in a real factory may require thousands of lines. The best mix is where two certain lines
cross, which is where two quantities are equal.

By adding, subtracting, testing, and repeating, the
computer can do the same job. Instead of drawing the
lines, the programmer tells it to vary the numbers and
then compare them all with each other again, thousands of times, until it finds the best mix.

Mathematical models also create other kinds of
artificial experience. For example, the force against
an airplane wing varies with the shape of the wing,
the speed, and other things that can all be expressed
as numbers. Putting all those numbers together in the

right way creates a mathematical model of the wing. The computer can store the model in memory. The programmer can tell it to change certain numbers—for example, increase the speed—and then compare all the numbers with each other again.

The computer is "flying" the new wing mathematically to see how it will work before it is even built.

Anything that can be expressed in numbers can be modeled in the computer—things too small to see, such as the way molecules move during a chemical change, and things too big to comprehend, such as the way the weather starts near the North Pole and swirls around the world, changing to the touch of land and water, sun and season, and, as it passes, creating its own model in a tree trunk.

Machines are built to extend the abilities of people. Cars extend the ability to walk, trucks to carry, and television to see. By doing arithmetic in millionths of a second, the computer extends our ability to think.

But creating artificial experience is beyond that. We live at the instant we call "now." The past is gone forever. The future is never here, except as we can manipulate our models to answer the "what if" questions. Those answers help us to discover the distant past and to create our own future.

10
MAN VERSUS MACHINES

How would you teach a blind man to play checkers?
First, you could number all the playing squares on
the checkerboard:

Then you could name the men—Red A, Black A, Red B, Black B, etc.

Now explain the rules to the blind man; set up the board and make a move:

Tell the blind man, "Red I to 18."

He might answer, "Black L to 15," and you could move for him.

You might move Red K to 20, he might move Black K to 14, and so on. If the blind man had a remarkable memory, he could play the whole game.

The computer has a perfect memory. "Red I to 18" is easy to "say" on the computer's input typewriter. A set of simple rules for checkers is not much more complicated than the rules for keeping the miniplex stock record:

- select a man;
- add three or four to the number of his square;
- test: is that square occupied?

- if yes, select another man and test again;
- if no, send a message to the typewriter ("Black L to 15," for example).

Of course, just following these rules, the computer would always make the first open move, and so you could beat it every time.

Back in the 1950's an IBM mathematician named Arthur L. Samuel programmed a computer to play checkers, following simple rules. Then he added some instructions to make the computer:

- test one possible move against another to select the better one—jump an enemy man if you can, for example;
- store the way the men were lined up each time a move worked and each time it failed;
- test every move first against those patterns—don't make the same mistake again, and watch for opportunities to repeat what works.

Dr. Samuel had programmed a computer to learn. Soon it was beating him.

Why not? You and I—and Dr. Samuel—learned to play checkers the same way. We memorized the rules of the game and then, by playing, learned which moves win and which lose, so that we can repeat winning moves and avoid losing ones.

That's also the way we learn more complicated things. If a computer can learn how to play checkers better than the man who "taught" it, can computers eventually learn to do everything better than people?

The computer can remember better and more accurately and follow complex instructions more reliably. It can even learn from its own experience. It can have purpose—win the game, fly to the moon—and it has no fears, hopes, doubts, or wishes to distract it from that purpose.

Does it think? That depends on what you mean. The computer can go beyond following instructions; it can change them and even create its own. It can make decisions, and when it doesn't have enough information to decide, it can ask questions about how and what.

But it can never wonder.

The computer can develop answers, but it can never discover meanings. It can make logical decisions, but not value judgments. It can calculate faster than a thousand mathematicians, but it cannot care about the results.

Human thinking mixes caring—hopes and fears and other emotions—into the logic. Sometimes those emotions get in our way, as when you worry so much about a test that you can't remember what you know. The computer never worries or forgets. But emotions also lead us to ideas and insights beyond the connections of simple logic—and beyond the reach of the computer.

Three hundred years ago a man named Johannes Kepler looked up at the night sky, wondering. After twenty years of study, he defined the way the planets wheel around the sun in great elliptical paths, hurrying up as they pass close to the sun and then slowing down as they move away. He upset ideas two thousand years old, and out of his doubt and wonder he created a new logic that computers follow today as they send a spacecraft out from this planet to meet another.

The spacecraft started a long time ago—before the computer, before Kepler, even before the ancient Britons hauled huge boulders onto an empty plain to mark the positions of the sun and the moon and the stars. The spacecraft started when the first man looked at the night sky and wondered why—which is a question the computer can't ask.

GLOSSARY

ABACUS: an ancient device for solving arithmetical problems by counting beads that are strung on wires.

ANALOG COMPUTER: a machine that solves mathematical problems by representing numbers by something that can be measured, such as electrical voltage, length, rotations, etc. It sets up a model that is *analogous* to the problem. For example, an automobile speedometer computes speed by measuring the rate of rotation of a shaft. An analog computer measures continuously; a digital computer counts discretely, one at a time.

BINARY: having two conditions or possibilities. A switch is a binary device; it is either on or off.

BINARY ARITHMETIC: a way of counting and solving arithmetical problems using only two number symbols, 0 and 1. Digital computers are made of components that are either on or off, and so these computers use binary arithmetic.

CIRCUIT: path of electricity.

CODE: a system of numbers each of which has a pre-assigned meaning. The instructions to a computer are translated into the numbers, or code, that control the circuits inside it.

COIL: a spiral of wire used in electrical circuits.

CORE: a tiny ring of magnetic material inside a computer that is magnetized in one direction or the other to store a 1 or a 0.

DATA: facts, information.

DATA PROCESSING: using computing machines to produce records and solve mathematical problems.

DIGIT: symbol used in counting; a number; 0, 1, 2 . . . 9, are decimal digits; 0 and 1 are also binary digits.

DIGITAL COMPUTER: a machine that solves problems by changing them into numerical representations. An electronic digital computer uses pulses of electricity, which it counts discretely, one at a time (an analog computer measures continuously). A digital computer can perform logical operations on the data it receives and also on the instructions stored inside it.

ELECTRONIC: referring to the flow of electrons. Conventional electrical machines use electricity to operate mechanical parts; electronic machines use smaller, often minute, amounts of electricity for a wide variety of tasks. Electronic devices use electron tubes or transistors.

ENIAC: one of the first electronic digital computers. The letters stand for Electronic Numerical Integrator and Calculator.

INPUT: information fed into the computer.

INSTRUCTIONS: set of symbols or numbers that control the circuits inside the computer to "tell" it what to do step by step.

INVENTORY: a record of things used in a business—parts, products, supplies, etc.—showing how many are on hand, how many are on order, and other information.

KEYBOARD: a set of marked levers, such as a typewriter keyboard, that an operator depresses to record information.

KEYPUNCH: a machine the size of a small desk with a keyboard similar to that of a typewriter that records information by punching holes in cards. The holes are positioned according to a code that the computer translates into numbers and letters.

LIGHT PEN: a device shaped like a pen, wired to the TV-like screen that is the "window into the computer." As information from the computer appears on the screen, the operator points the light pen to signal what he wants to change. The light from the screen activates the light pen, which sends a signal back to the computer. Light pens can be used to instruct the computer to draw shapes in light on the screen.

MAGNETIC DISK: a metal platter that looks like a big phonograph record, coated on both sides with magnetic material, used for storing information as tiny magnetic spots.

MAGNETIC DRUM: a large metal cylinder coated with magnetic material, used for storing information as tiny magnetic spots.

MAGNETIC SPOT: a tiny individual magnet on the surface of magnetic material. A computer reads and writes information on magnetic tape, disks and drums in the form of magnetic spots.

MAGNETIC TAPE: metal or plastic tape, coated with magnetic material, used for storing information as tiny magnetic spots.

MAGNETISM: the particles of certain metals, called magnetic materials, can be made to line up facing the same way; such materials attract or repel other magnetic materials nearby. The invisible force is magnetism; the material that has this property is called a magnet. A magnet moved past a closed coil of wire causes electricity to flow in the coil; this also works in reverse: electricity flowing in a coil creates a magnetic effect and can make a magnet of, or a magnetic spot on, nearby magnetic material.

MAXIPACK: an imaginary product in this book.

MEMORY: in a computer, a device for storing information and instructions as binary numbers.

MINIPLEX: a part inside the maxipack, an imaginary product in this book.

MODEL: one version of a product; for example, the maxipack, an imaginary product in this book, is made in two models, plainjane and streamliner. Also, a representation of a device, a process, or an idea; a mathematical model is a representation using numbers, and a computer can vary those numbers automatically to create many different models until it finds the best possible one.

ORDER POINT: the quantity available of an item of inventory at which more units of the item are ordered to refill the inventory before all the units are used.

PLAINJANE: a low-cost model of the maxipack, an imaginary product in this book.

PROCESSING: information going through logical operations inside the computer according to a series of instructions stored in the computer's memory.

PROGRAM: a set of step-by-step coded instructions that tells the computer exactly how to handle every choice that might arise in dealing with a problem or operation.

PULSE: a momentary flow of electricity.

STREAMLINER: a fancy, more expensive model of the maxipack, an imaginary product in this book.

INDEX